Dearest John —

You Are Amazing

Thank you for the

Wonderful Difference

You make in this

World!

Love — Cindy

2/29/16

Always Hope

True stories of ordinary people overcoming extraordinary odds

**compiled by
Cindy Cline-Flores**

**with a Foreword by
Ray Bradbury**

**and photographs by
Alisa Murray**

HopeFull Enterprises

Always Hope; True stories of ordinary people overcoming extraordinary odds

Compiled by Cindy Cline-Flores

©2010 by Cindy Cline-Flores

HopeFull Enterprises

ISBN: 978-0-615-35301-2

www.AlwaysHopeBook.com

Printed in the United States of America

Editing, Layout, and Graphic Design
by
Schmidt, Kaye & Company
Waller, Texas USA

Contents

Author Ray Bradbury

Foreword

Joy Is The Grace We Say To God
by
RAY BRADBURY

Glancing through this incredible book, I am reminded of two things: A poem I read many years ago with the line, "Joy is the grace we say to God." The other thing is an Egyptian myth. I'll attend to the myth first.

The myth relates the simple fact that when you die and go to heaven, the god of the dead, standing at the gate, will test you with only one question. The question Is: In this life, did you know enthusiasm? If the answer is no, you go straight to hell. If the answer is yes, you pass easily through the gates to eternal celebrations of the future.

So, what you have here are photographs and words of many people that have many reasons not to be enthusiastic, and yet they reach out toward life with that vitality which can only be named as the enthusiasm that will pass them through the gates one day.

Finally, to return to the poem, all of us, regardless of our stature, and whether we've had good lives or bad, feel this incredible joy at morning to wake and realize we have yet another day to live and celebrate, because we are all grateful for the gift, whether it is large or small, whether it is cramped or whether it is free.

These people, then, to me, represent that joy which is the grace that we give God in return for life and, finally, shining in their faces, there is a quiet enthusiasm that cannot be quenched.

So I think I have named my two reactions to all of these amazing people who are teaching me, with their words and faces, how to behave toward the life that I live.

~ Ray Bradbury, 2009

Dedicated
In Loving Memory
to
Marion Charles
1945 ~ 1997

Cindy Cline-Flores

A young beauty, alive with dreams and living in

Magical Times

Soylent Green wrap party
Edward G. Robinson, Leigh Taylor Young,
Marion Charles, Charlton Heston

Dedication

The inspiration for creating this book originally came from my older sister, Marion. She was my role model, my mentor, and my best friend. Marion was a successful actress and model, working in New York and California in the late 60s and the 70s. She was the Chiquita Banana girl, and was featured in numerous other television commercials. Marion appeared in the hit movie *Soylent Green*, which starred Charlton Heston and Edward G. Robinson, and had a role in another movie titled *Ginger In the Morning*, starring Sissy Spacek. She frequently appeared in popular television shows of the period, such as *Love, American Style, Dragnet*, and *Barnaby Jones*. She even appeared on *The Johnny Carson Show*.

Then in the mid 80s, a head-on auto accident in the mountains of California left Marion comatose and paralyzed. Her friends called and told my mom and me that we needed to come right away, because the doctors held out little hope of Marion surviving. She was in a coma when she arrived at the hospital, completely unresponsive to her friends or anyone. When Mom and I first walked into the ICU, we were beyond shocked. The only sound was the constant pshhh-pshhh of the respirator. Marion's face was badly cut, covered with stitches, and her head was half-shaven. It seemed that tubes beyond count were coming out of every part of her body. My first impression was that she had passed away; she didn't even appear to be breathing to me. Our mom marched right past me and all the machines and monitors as if they weren't even there, gently placed her hand on Marion's head, and started whispering in her ear, "My baby. My sweet, sweet little baby girl." Immediately, Marion's heart rate started rising, and her chest started moving up and down. She was breathing so hard that bubbles started pouring out of her breathing tube. Mom said, "Marion, if you can hear me, squeeze my hand." Marion gave a tiny, gentle squeeze.

This was the beginning of a nine-month hospital stay, and a lifelong healing journey. Mom and I sat for hours and days on end, watching her on the breathing machine. The doctors told us that she probably would not regain full consciousness, but Mom and I knew differently. From the time we were children, Marion and I loved to sing together. Now, as she lay so horribly wounded, I would sing her our favorite songs, and she would blow little bubbles from her breathing tube. I knew she was hearing me, as her lips would move slightly as I sang. The doctors said it was just muscle reflex, but Mom and I knew differently. Marion might have been in a place beyond our understanding, but she was still here with us, fighting to sing, and to live.

Over the next months and years, Marion continued to amaze the doubters in the medical profession. She did come out of her coma. Initially, however, she was paralyzed, could not speak because of severe damage to her vocal cords, and had suffered significant brain damage. One day in the hospital, Mom and I saw her big toe move. Once again, we were told it was only muscle reflex, but again, we knew differently. On another day, we heard her voice, but were told she would not be able to talk in an understandable voice. Mom's and my faith, however, remained unshaken. Marion had repeatedly amazed the doctors, and we just knew she would do so again. And amaze them, she did!

After nine months of hospitalization and extensive therapy, Marion was released from the hospital, and returned home to Texas. After many years of therapy, Marion became able to walk with a cane, and she most certainly could talk! Eventually, she even managed to drive a car and live on her own, without the constant assistance that the doctors had told us she would always require. During this time, I searched and searched for books and stories to share with her, stories that would be inspiring – inspiring enough to help her through the long recovery road ahead, and inspiring enough for her to want to live.

Back in Houston, my sister tried very hard to make new friends and to gain employment. Over the years, and faced with frustration at every turn, the struggle eventually became too much for her, and she lost all hope. In April of 1997, she ended her life. I wanted to shout at the world, "Why didn't you look in her eyes when talking to her? Why didn't you treat her with the respect, and care, and kindness she deserved?" But even then, I knew the answer. Many people couldn't really be present with Marion because they were afraid, as if by relating to her, they might somehow be faced with the same challenges that she faced. And I am sure that others felt awkward, unsure of the "right" way to deal with her. When my sister ended her life, I felt that a part of me had died with her. I felt like there was a huge, black hole in my soul. I would cry myself to sleep each night, and awaken each morning to more tears. I wondered if I would have the strength to live through her death, and I especially wondered how my mom would live through the death of her child. When Marion died, she took part of us with her.

Some years later, my nephew and his wife were involved in a serious motorcycle accident. While they both suffered severe injuries, his wife's leg had to be amputated. They have two young children. As I walked into the ICU to see my nephew's wife, who was in critical condition, I tried to think – as I had with my sister Marion – of every positive story I could imagine, to tell her to give her hope and help lift her spirits. I recalled the story of Ray Charles, who managed to overcome extreme poverty, blindness, and drug addiction to become a true icon in the music industry, and beyond that, an inspiration to all who heard his music, even if they knew nothing about the obstacles he had overcome. His ability to laugh at his predicament truly inspired me beyond words, and I applaud him for his strength.

Then, just months later, my youngest sister, who has two very young children, was diagnosed with a very rare form of cancer. Once again, my world was shaken, and I tried to think of every possible story of hope, of people beating the odds of "incurable diseases." Once again, I wished for a book that would serve as inspiration.

I kept finding myself in situations where loved ones and friends were facing difficult challenges in their lives. I wanted to leave them with an inspiring book – a book filled with actual stories of people who have been through, and overcome, trauma – a book that would give them hope!

Then one day, I was standing at the water cooler at my workplace, again wishing for such a book, when I noticed a poster above the cooler that read, "Be The Change You Wish To See," a quote by Gandhi. It became clear that the book did exist; it just hadn't been written yet. I decided right then that it was my job to create this book – a book to give hope and inspiration to all people, and especially those who find themselves facing life's most difficult situations. This is what I call a God Job!

This book is a collection of essays describing the journeys that these brave souls have taken (and on which they continue each day). The stories are about ordinary people who have not only faced their fears, but have gone on to see the beauty life offers to those who take the time to see and consider the wonders all around them. By taking the time, and opening their eyes, hearts, and souls, these "ordinary" people have become quite extraordinary. Working on this project, and getting to know some of the people who offered their stories, has touched me on a very deep soul level. To say that I feel honored and blessed to bring their stories forward would be a gross understatement. In the most profound sense, they are my heroes.

It is my deepest desire that by offering a glimpse into the lives of these not-so-ordinary heroes, this book will raise awareness about people with disabilities, and serve as a source of hope and inspiration to all who read it – especially those who find themselves on a challenging journey of their own.

~ Cindy Cline-Flores

Kristina Thorson
Photo by Alisa Murray

Cindy Cline-Flores

One Beautiful
Sunday Afternoon

One beautiful Sunday afternoon, my children and I returned home from church to find my husband Ric finishing up some minor maintenance on our newly acquired motorcycle. As I prepared lunch, Ric suggested that he and I take a motorcycle ride. I had never been very fond of riding motorcycles, due to my fear of accidents, so I told him I wasn't sure I wanted to go. Throughout the day, Ric continued to ask me to ride with him. He can be quite persistent, and I knew he was really looking forward to our spending some time alone together. Finally, I relented, but even after we dropped off our children at Ric's grandparents' house, I still had reservations about taking this motorcycle ride.

"Why don't you just go, and I'll stay home," I suggested one last time. But because I could tell Ric really wanted me to come along, I climbed onto the bike. "If I break my leg on this ride, I'm gonna kick your rear end," I promised. Little did I know how true those words would ring for us both.

Our ride actually began quite nicely. It was a balmy spring day in late March. The weather felt pleasantly warm, and all of the plants were in bloom. As we rode along, my fears eased, calmed by the breathtaking scenery and the reassurance that my husband is a very good driver. I'd ridden with him before and nothing had ever happened. To my surprise, I was really enjoying myself.

A little later, my husband found a relatively desolate area and pulled off the road to answer nature's call. Upon his return to the motorcycle, we walked around for a few more minutes to stretch our legs. As we climbed back on his bike, my husband told me that his new helmet was bothering him. We discussed what we might do about it, came to no conclusion, and resumed our ride. Moments later, my feelings of enjoyment gave way to fear. I watched the road flying by beneath us, and thought about how easy it would be for us to lay the bike down. I couldn't get the fear out of my mind. Though it consumed me, I didn't tell my husband. I told myself that I was just blowing my fear out of proportion, but the feeling did not go away. I began praying to God over and over again to protect us and keep us safe.

I vaguely remember our being hit by the car. I recall feeling as though my breath had been knocked out of me instantly. I remember flipping in the air over the grass. I knew it was grass, because all I could see was green. In mid-spin, I wondered if this were really happening, yet I knew it was, and felt sick in the pit of my stomach. It seemed as though I would flip forever, and I wondered if I'd ever stop. When I finally did stop rolling, I wished that I hadn't. Only then did I feel excruciating pain in my right leg. I'd never before experienced such agony. I began screaming for someone – anyone – to help me. I stared into the sky, crying out, "God, please help me." I knew that if anyone had the power to help me, it would be Him. It would have to be God. I would soon find out that He had helped me, and would continue to do so.

The lady who hit us was the first to offer assistance. As I lay on the side of the road, she stayed by my side, trying her best to comfort me. The pain was unbearable, and I felt terrified. I begged for relief from the pain, and kept praying to God for help. In what seemed only moments later, an older man approached and asked if he could pray for me. I clearly remember telling him yes. In his prayer he told me that I would feel calm and peaceful, and my pain would ease. His prayer relaxed me. As he finished, I felt peaceful, and believed I was going to be all right.

When the paramedics arrived they asked me questions to assess my state of mind. I had become so relaxed after the man had prayed for me that I really wished the paramedics would forego the questioning and let me rest. Bystanders were so amazed by the emotional transformation that they began looking for the man who had prayed for me to thank him. They were unable to find him, and insisted that no one had left the accident scene. I will forever be thankful to the mysterious man that God sent to help me that day.

My husband and I were reunited in the Life Flight helicopter. While lying side-by-side on stretchers, he held my hand the entire way to the hospital. Having him next to me helped tremendously.

At the hospital, we were both wheeled into the emergency room. The last thing I remember was being asked by a dark-haired doctor if I needed pain medicine. "Yes," I said. Approximately two weeks later, I woke up in intensive care.

For the two months I remained in the hospital, I received tremendous support from my family, especially my mother, who stayed by my side the entire time. My entire family took turns coming to see me. Throughout my stay, I don't ever recall being at the hospital alone. My husband's grandparents kept Emily and Jacob while Ric recovered at home. Even though he had been injured pretty severely, he came to see me as often as possible.

My injuries required numerous surgeries, but despite the doctors' best efforts, I ended up losing my right leg below the knee.

Prior to the accident, my husband and I had wanted to have one more baby. I really had a feeling that we were to have a girl, and had even picked out her name: Sarah Ann. Approximately eleven months after being released from the hospital, I learned that I was pregnant. Because my mother had seen how much I'd gone through after the accident, I was afraid to tell her that I was going to have another baby. I was concerned that she would be worried as to how I would care for the baby with my injuries. I took the coward's way out and called my sister, Teresa, to ask her to break the news to our mother.

I dreaded the phone call that I was sure I would receive from my worried mother. The phone rang, and as I had expected, it was my mother, but she wasn't worried at all. She told me she thought I was going to have a girl named

Kristina, with Emily, Jacob and Sarah Ann
Photo by Alisa Murray

Sarah Ann. Her words shocked me. I had not told my mother of our plan to have another baby, or so I thought. She said that while I was in the hospital I frequently told her that I knew I was supposed to have one more baby – a girl named Sarah Ann. She said I would cry and tell her that I was afraid that my injuries had made it impossible for me to have this baby. She said she consoled me in those moments by telling me that I would still be able to. I must have been pretty heavily sedated, because I don't remember those conversations at all, but they obviously did take place.

As I write this, I am seven months pregnant, and the baby is due January 13, 2004. An ultrasound has confirmed that Ric and I are going to have a baby girl. Our entire family is eagerly awaiting Sarah Ann's arrival.

Although my conversations in the hospital remain a blur, I recall the warnings God gave me as I rode on the back of the motorcycle. To my surprise, Ric has since told me that the day of the accident he also had feelings that we should turn the motorcycle around. But like me, he pushed the thoughts to the back of his mind. If either of us had voiced our concerns, we would have avoided the accident.

God had tried to warn us, but we didn't listen. He couldn't change fate at that point, but he truly protected us. The fact that we are both still here with our precious children, Emily and Jacob, and soon-to-be Sarah Ann, is proof of that. Our journey from that beautiful Sunday afternoon to this point has been hard at times, but it has opened my eyes to many, many wonderful things at the same time. We are truly blessed.

~ *Kristina Thorson*

Aaron at his favorite place — the beach
Photo by Joe Flores

Cindy Cline-Flores

Shark Attack:
The Aaron Perez Story

I believe that each of our lives is touched by angels, usually when we least expect it. Some may arrive offering challenges so great that we may wonder whether we can survive the encounter, while others bless us so deeply that they wash away any doubt that there is, indeed, a kind and benevolent Creator. Aaron Perez is one of the latter. Of this, I am certain. While I found his story inspiring, and felt it belonged in this book, I was not prepared for the feelings I experienced when I first came face to face with this remarkable little boy, and saw the strength behind his gentle eyes. But before I get completely ahead of myself, I guess it would help if I told you his story, and let you decide for yourself.

Life for eleven-year-old Aaron Perez was pretty ordinary that summer of 2004. For a boy who loved to fish as much as he did, living on the Gulf Coast in Freeport, Texas was perfect. At every possible opportunity, you would find him wading through the surf, rod in hand, trying to snag the speckled trout, "specks," with his mom and dad. Actually, he and his dad did most of the fishing, but Mom was an enthusiastic supporter, and the whole family enjoyed those long summer days on the beach. And when Aaron couldn't get to the water, he would scan the television cable channels for fishing and wildlife shows. One particular show had really caught his attention that week in mid-July: a documentary on sharks. Like everybody else who lives on the Gulf, Aaron had heard of the shark attacks that had occurred on the Gulf. He knew the predators were out there, but wasn't particularly concerned. Just the same, he watched the show, fascinated, learning about the habits of sharks, the myths that surrounded them, and even what to do in the unlikely event that he encountered one himself. Little did he know that barely a week later, what he saw in the show would become altogether too real to him.

The 25th of July was a fairly typical Sunday for Aaron and his family. He and his father, Blas, and his mother, Thelma, spent the afternoon at the beach with family friends, Don and Jan Townes. While the "boys" busied themselves with the task of depleting the Gulf's speck population, the "girls" stayed back onshore, preparing for the watermelon feast that they would all enjoy as soon as the fishermen decided to take a break. At about six o'clock in the evening, after spending a couple of fruitless hours casting, but getting no bites, the guys came in. Anyone who has spent even a few hours baking in the Texas sun knows full well how tempting a cool slice of watermelon can be, and the guys were no different. Still, after standing around for awhile, eating and laughing about the dismal catch so far, they decided to give the fish one more chance before calling it a day.

Once they entered the water, it seemed as if they were in a whole different world. While the wind was as still as it had been before, and the water was smooth, uninterrupted by anything resembling waves, the fish had arrived, and they were hungry! The guys were pulling in fish as quickly as they could cast their lines. This was what fishing was all about. Then, as suddenly as it had begun, the frenzy ended. The fish seemed to disappear. Blas turned to Aaron, who was standing a dozen yards away, and asked him where all the fish had gone. Looking down, Aaron saw that the specks were all around him, and wondered why they had suddenly gotten so still and stopped biting. He actually reached down and plucked one from the water to show his father. Then, to his horror, he got the answer to his question.

The first thing Aaron felt was a searing pain in his right leg. All of a sudden, the documentary he had seen days before snapped back into his consciousness; he was being attacked by a seven-foot bull shark. As Aaron screamed for his father and struggled to pull free, the shark released his leg, only to clamp down on his right arm, nearly severing it. As his father and Don Townes ran toward him, Aaron lashed out at his attacker, smashing his fists into the shark's sensitive gills, as he had learned from the documentary. Blas Perez, normally a remarkably gentle man, bounded toward his son, screaming and pummeling the beast with the only weapon at hand – his fishing rod. Don Townes arrived immediately afterward, joining Blas in his frenzied assault. Finally, after what seemed like hours, but was actually about ten minutes, the shark released the boy and swam away. Don scooped up the horribly wounded Aaron, and the men ran toward the shore, screaming for Thelma Perez and Don's wife, Jan, to bring the truck.

The next moments were a blur for the families, with Blas driving, as he put it, "like a maniac," while Thelma called 911. They were stopped by a policeman who had observed Blas' erratic driving, but upon seeing the situation, the officer pulled Blas from the driver's seat, pushed him in the back seat of the truck, and drove to the Freeport Fire

Cindy Cline-Flores

Department station, where paramedics awaited them. Fortunately, they had already summoned a Life Flight helicopter from Memorial Hermann Children's Hospital in Houston. The paramedics knew that if the boy's life – and his arm – were to be saved, he would have to get to the hospital quickly, as he had already lost a great deal of blood.

Once the paramedics had Aaron stabilized, the helicopter arrived. The moment that the helicopter's crew, Jeff Cobb and Melissa Kendrick, saw Aaron, they knew that he was an extraordinary eleven-year-old. Where they had expected the child to be frantic, as is typical when children suffer such extreme trauma, the boy seemed frightened, but calm. He asked Melissa if he were going to die, or going to lose his arm. She did her best to reassure him, though she wondered herself whether her assurances were true. At one point, Aaron asked the attendants to pray with him, and they knew he was truly an exceptional child – in the best sense of the word. Throughout the flight to Houston, Aaron clutched Melissa's hand tightly, as if her hand were his only lifeline, and letting go would mean his death. Even when they landed at the hospital, and Melissa had to let go of the boy's hand to pull his gurney from the aircraft, he struggled to find her hand again. When the other crewman, Jeff, offered his own hand to the boy, Aaron pulled back. He wanted Melissa and only Melissa. Amid the near-panic of the situation, Aaron's reaction brought the crew some much-needed levity. It seemed to Melissa that this horribly injured little boy was actually seeing to the emotional comfort of the very people who were, at this moment, charged with saving his life.

Once inside the hospital, Aaron was seen by Dr. Emmanuel Melissinos, clinical professor of surgery at the University of Texas Medical School at Houston. Dr. Melissinos was one of the finest in the profession; he had started a microsurgery program at Memorial Hermann Children's Hospital twenty-five years before. It was he who would be performing the surgery to try to save the boy's arm. Despite his expertise, Dr. Melissinos was somewhat doubtful about the outcome, as Aaron's arm had been all but severed, with all the arteries, tendons, and nerves detached, along with the muscle. Literally all that held the boy's forearm in place were the bones, which had been splintered by the shark's powerful jaws. Even amid his doubts, the surgeon prepared himself for what was destined to be a very long night in the operating room. As you would imagine, it was an even longer night in the waiting room for Blas and Thelma and the Townes.

Come morning, an exhausted Dr. Melissinos entered the waiting room to give the parents the news: it looked as if the arm had been saved, and that Aaron was doing well in recovery. The doctor had expected to find the four adults awaiting word, but what he actually encountered was a room filled to overflowing, with friends, neighbors, and many members of the Perez' church family, all hovering around, offering whatever support they could give to the worried parents. What Blas and Thelma didn't know was that some of the church members had already gone to their home and cleaned the house and, especially, the truck, which had been splattered with the evidence of Aaron's experience.

The hospital's medical staff were amazed at Aaron's rate of progress, and after a week, he was released to go home to continue his healing. Much to Thelma's surprise – and Blas' dismay – Aaron was actually chomping at the bit to get back in the water, to his favorite pastime. Blas, on the other hand, didn't know if he could ever go near the water again. It wasn't a fear for his own safety that would keep him away, but rather the horrible memory of a father who has watched his child suffer, and almost die. And there was the inevitable feeling of guilt: the unsettling thought that he could have, should have, done something to prevent the attack. Though Thelma repeatedly assured him that he was blameless and did everything he could to help Aaron, Blas was still tormented by that guilt.

As the weeks passed, Aaron returned to see Dr. Melissinos, who was quite pleased with the boy's progress. Though he knew that Aaron faced many months of painful therapy, and that the pain the boy felt would intensify as the nerves in his arm healed, he felt certain that Aaron would regain the use of his hand. For the time being, however, the doctor felt that it would be unwise to start school before further healing had taken place.

Though Aaron's spirit was strong and his optimism unflagging, the trauma had left marks that ran deeper than his physical injuries. He had nightmares, frequently waking his parents up with his screaming. His mother said that on these occasions Aaron did not believe he was merely having a bad dream; he truly thought something was in the room attacking him. That was how real, and how deep, the trauma still was to him. It would take a while for him to get over this.

For most little boys, the end of summer is a sad thing, with leisure and freedom being replaced by tests, homework, and countless hours spent indoors, which is the last place they would want to be. But Aaron was anxious to get back to his friends, and grew increasingly restless as the days passed. Finally, after weeks that seemed like years, Dr. Melissinos decided that Aaron was well enough to join his classmates. On his first day of school, Aaron was overwhelmed – and quite pleased – by all the attention he got. All of the students and teachers had followed his story on television, and had a seemingly unending stream of questions, which Aaron was more than happy to answer.

Eventually, Aaron did return to Bryan Beach, to the very place where the stuff of his – and his father's – nightmare had been born. Watching him run and cavort about in the water, it is hard to believe that he could return to this place, but return, he has. Looking at Aaron's and Blas' faces, one would hardly believe that it was the boy, rather than the man, who had been attacked. Yet as the hours passed, the shadows seemed to pass from both of them, and it was obvious that the long process of their souls' healing had begun.

Naturally, Aaron faces a long period of physical recovery, including frequent and painful sessions of physical therapy, before gaining full use of his arm, and is still not sure whether he will regain his ability to play the piano. But in spite of the trials he has been subjected to, as well as those that still face him, he remains a cheerful boy, who eagerly looks forward to each day. Perhaps we adults could do well to learn from this incredibly gentle, yet profoundly strong child, and discover that, despite the setbacks and suffering we encounter, we must always hope. It has been told that Jesus held a deep affinity for fishermen. After spending even a little time with Aaron, I can certainly understand why. For in those brief moments when his presence touched my life, my own sense of hope, and my faith in the inherent goodness of life, has been renewed, my faith rekindled.
~ *Cindy Cline-Flores*

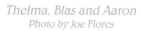

Thelma, Blas and Aaron
Photo by Joe Flores

Deborah Buks with her two sons, Joseph and Isaac
Photo by Alisa Murray

Cindy Cline-Flores

The Gift

Everything has changed since I was diagnosed with sarcoma in April of 2002. I look back over the past years at the little things. I find that I now discipline my children with infinitely more patience, because at their very tender ages, this could be the last – or the only – interaction with me that they remember. I know that at any moment, I could be whisked off to the emergency room, my white count so low that a simple cold kills me. So I think twice about how I'm going to react to yogurt splashed on the new paint job in the kitchen. Suddenly, I'm just so thrilled to be here for it that I'm not willing to give away my energy to anger and little upsets. I just don't have that luxury. So I think I'm a much better parent than I would have been, had I never been diagnosed with cancer.

It's interesting. I'd never have thought when I got diagnosed that I would look back and say cancer is one of the biggest blessings of my life. It's devastating in the beginning. When I first got diagnosed, I thought my opponent was death. I found myself in a battle with an invisible enemy whose weapons and tactics were unknown and unpredictable. How do you fight such an enemy? Then, as you go through the process, you realize that you really can't have that kind of mind-set. It dawns on you that everybody is going to die. You find yourself thinking of death, not as the enemy, but as a vehicle of passage, a newness, an opportunity, and as a chapter of your soul's life. There's a real freedom in that. And once you have faced death, facing life looks a lot easier. I can see what's going on in life. I can see human behavior and things that people do that used to drive me crazy and think, "It's okay." I feel like I can manage all the things that are in the knowable realm. Things that stressed me out before really don't have that much power over me any more. It's not that the world around me has changed; what has changed is my perspective.

Of course, finding this new way of looking at things didn't occur instantaneously. While I was going through the fear and anger stages, other cancer survivors – people that I didn't really know very well – started showing up at my house for a visit when they got the news of my diagnosis. We suddenly had a lot of traffic in the house, and everybody who came over would tell me, "You can get through this." They tried to give me this perspective, but in the beginning, I couldn't get it. I couldn't even hear it yet. However, it was a ray of hope during that long time before I was able see how many good things had come to me from my cancer.

A lot of people die in a car wreck or make their transition suddenly in some other way, without any warning. But in my case, I got this outpouring and showering of unbelievable infinite love and care-taking from people all around me, which was awesome – even better than being at your own funeral! Most people don't get the benefit of all that; some don't even get the chance to say goodbye.

I've never been sick before, and never thought of myself as a "sick person." I don't know what I thought. At some level, I guess I perceived that that there were sick-people and not-sick-people; that sick-people had always been sick, or that they were just the kind of people that got sick. My personal experience with sickness was limited to seasonal allergies, a tonsillectomy, and two C-sections. I've never had people take care of me, because I never needed it. I've had to learn not to view being cared for as a weakness, but to allow myself to receive and realize that receiving is actually a form of generosity; that letting others give to you brings them the purest kind of joy.

Some days are very hard, and a lot of days, I'm still very scared. When I find myself in that frightened state of mind, I have to take a deep breath and ask myself if I am in the here and now, or somewhere in the shadows of what I fear might be my future. Usually, if I'm afraid, it's because someone I know or someone in my support group has passed, had another surgery, lost another limb, or gotten a bad prognosis. Bad things are happening around me, and I become afraid that those bad things might happen to me, too. But if I really look at it, I see my thoughts are not in the present. If I'm upset, I'm either fearing what might happen or grieving about what has happened or what I've lost. I'm definitely not being right here, at this moment, in this breath. The only thing I've found to bring myself back to center is to ask myself "Are you being here now? Because if not, you're missing it. This is your whole life. You've been given this gift of life. The past is gone. The future is not here yet. This moment is it…. this moment is the only life you really have, and now you're wasting it." When this awareness finally sinks in, I move from a place of fear to one of profound gratitude, thankful for the moment, and determined not to waste it.

I say if you're grieving, grieve. I feel that being at cause, on purpose – at whatever I do – is the right thing. If I feel like being a couch potato because I'm too weak to move, then baby, I'm going to be the biggest couch-potato, surrounded-by-my-favorite-foods-and-remote-control that you ever saw. If I need to grieve and cry for things that are not going to be – like when the after-effects of chemotherapy have made sure that I'm not going to have that job, or that I can't take care of my own babies – I cry about it and I don't make apologies for my tears. When well-meaning people tell me to cheer up, I say, "Hey, I'll be cheered up when I'm cheered up. There will be a time when I'm in a happy place, and there are times when I'm in a sad place. I'm not going try to suppress it or bury it to make you feel more comfortable."

Sometimes, if I express my fears, people react by scolding me. For example, the other day my husband said, "You can't think like that! You can't attract those kind of thoughts."

And I said, "Don't go there with me, because if I get bad news tomorrow – or after the next CAT scan – then I'm going to get stuck with the thought that if I had not been afraid, and if I hadn't had those negative thoughts, I wouldn't have attracted this to myself. You know I'm doing everything I can. I'm taking every drug. I'm praying. I'm drinking water. I can't beat myself up for not doing cancer right enough." I say whatever you're feeling, really feel it. Then it can pass. But if you keep suppressing it and not allowing yourself to have those feelings, you'll just end up giving those fears more power, and you will suffer too much, and too long.

Someone asked me, "What makes you get up in the morning?" Huh? What makes me get up is that I'm a mother. I've got two very young children, so every morning there's somebody's little lips pressed right up against my ear saying, "Mommy, it's time to get up. It's a sunny day, it's not dark day anymore." I'm like every other mother on the planet. I have kids and they get up at daybreak! They don't know if you're sick. They don't care if you had a lumpectomy yesterday. Life goes on and they're still in the mood to play, which is great. I think if I'd been by myself through this, I'd probably be dead by now. I would probably have been way too much in my own head, in my thoughts. With kids, you don't have time to think.

I relish the moments when people talk about all their petty little stuff, because for so many months after I got diagnosed, all anybody wanted to talk to me about was cancer. Sometimes you just want to scream and say, "I'm still in here! I still think about the things I used to talk to you about. I still have a husband, and we still have a relationship, and that's a roller coaster if you're married. I still have parenting challenges. I still wish I didn't have a pot belly. I still wish I was a size six. I still think about that stuff." But when somebody else tells me about their stuff, for a brief moment, life is normal again, and I love those times. I think of that Latin phrase, *Dum Vita Est, Spes Est*. As long as there is life, there is hope. So if you're still here in hope and holding on to your hope, it's the best thing you can do for yourself.

The other day, I was meeting with a doctor who said there's a label in the medical community that they give certain patients – a phenomenon called "hardiness" or something like that. She said, "You strike me as one of those patients. Maybe you're where you're at (which is that I currently have no evidence of disease after initially being given very poor odds) because you do have that hardiness." She added, "So many people got the same drugs as you, they have the same stage of cancer, they have the same kind of disease, and yet they get the diagnosis and they go home prepared to die. And once their spirit dies, the body follows." While I appreciated that she saw me that way, I know that's not always the case. I mean, I know of people who are fighting like crazy – incredible, inspirational people – who you just think, "Man, you're making every minute of your life count, every time you open your mouth." I've met some wonderful people like that, whose bodies don't appear to be winning against the cells multiplying. It just seems to be a molecular thing happening.

I'm not afraid of death. I'm not afraid of making my transition. I'm okay with that, but I'm worried about my children. I want them to think I am the best mother they could ever have, and I want to be the one to raise them. But the only comfort and peace I've come to is that I think my soul chose this experience. I think all of our souls did. It seems to me that we started from a point of looking at the possible lives we could lead here on earth and said, "If I came into the world as this, then my soul will grow. I will be better. I will be closer to God. I will be more God-like." I don't know, but I think we chose this experience, and that sort of makes it okay. If my children chose this – whether to have a mother who either is victorious over cancer or one who passes from cancer – then they chose it because it was going to help them fulfill something in their spiritual life and in their soul. They're on their own divine plan or mission, and they're okay. It'll be all right, however it goes. That thought brings me peace. And I think that's the case in any situation.

I was talking to a woman yesterday who has gone through a difficult divorce. She told me that she has to put her little girl, age five, on an airplane once a month to go half way across the country all by herself to visit her father. The child is terrified each time she has to go, and she cries and screams, "I don't want to get on the airplane. Please Mommy, don't make me." But the woman knows that if she doesn't put her daughter on that plane, she will be violating a court order. She said that seeing her daughter's anguish is heartbreaking. So I told her about this philosophy, about our souls choosing the circumstances of our lives. And she said, "You know, at this moment, that idea brings me a lot of peace – to think that she chose this life, and she's fulfilling on what she came to fulfill on." Of course I don't know if it is true, but it makes me feel better! Cancer gave me that gift.
~ *Deborah Buks*

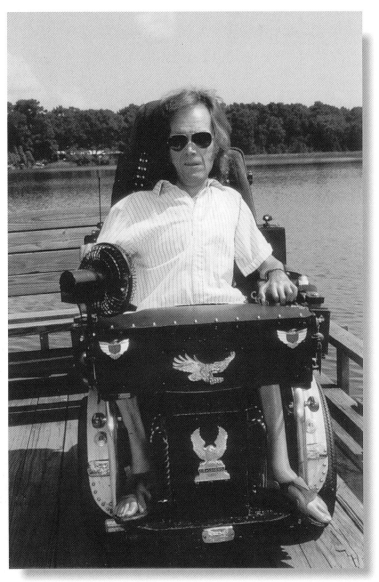

Rick Myers at the lake
Photo by Bob Grace

Cindy Cline-Flores

Boundless Mind

At sixteen months of age, I was diagnosed with Duchenne muscular dystrophy by one of the leading authorities on the condition in the United States. He informed my parents that I might not ever walk, and that it was unlikely I would live much into my teens. Instead, I would probably die of respiratory failure (pneumonia). Fortunately for my parents and me, doctors are not infallible.

When I was 21, doctors re-diagnosed my condition as spinal muscular atrophy, a progressive neuromuscular disease in which the motor nerves that affect muscle movement do not send a strong enough signal to keep the muscle healthy. As I write this, I am 56. I am the oldest individual in the entire Houston region of Texas who has this condition.

I have been clinically classified as totally physically disabled since birth, and have been dependent on others for my personal care my entire life. At this time, I'm barely able to operate a motorized wheelchair and can only feed myself with great effort, utilizing personally designed adaptive equipment. I could write volumes about my disability; however, by focusing on it I would be giving it energy. Experience taught me a long time ago to focus my energy on my abilities, rather than my disabilities. In spite of my severe physical limitations, I consider myself to be blessed, and have lived an interesting and fruitful life, with public recognition for a number of accomplishments:

1. I was recognized for scholastic achievement at both state and federal levels.
2. I graduated with a Master of Education degree in Vocational Rehabilitation Counseling from The University of Texas at Austin.
3. In 1992, I retired from employment after almost 20 years as a senior vocational rehabilitation counselor. To this date, I am the longest tenured employee in the history of the state vocational rehabilitation department who has a disability as severe as quadriplegia (impairment of all four extremities). At the time of my retirement, I was the only one of approximately five-hundred total counselors who were so disabled.

4. My interest in transportation problems of the severely mobility impaired have led to a number of developments:

 • I wrote a proposal and received a state grant for developing a prototype vehicle that could function as a cab for the general population, as well as for the severely mobility impaired (those in wheelchairs). Through contact with A.J. Foyt of A. J. Foyt Racing, I was privileged to get A. J.'s chief mechanic for design consultation. Many taxicab companies now use similar vehicles throughout the U.S.

 • General Motors Corporation sponsored a trip for me to Washington, D.C. to meet with senators and the then-president of General Motors, to get my input on a prototype transit vehicle for the general public as well as the mobility impaired. This concept vehicle has come to fruition, and it is currently mass produced.

 • During my conversation with the president of General Motors, and later through correspondence with him, I discussed my concept of developing a cross between a car and a van that would have the benefit of each and that might ultimately be modified for wheelchair accessibility. This concept was the forerunner of the minivan that was introduced to the public by the Chrysler Corporation several years later.

5. My interest in adaptive equipment for the severely physically disabled led to the attainment of my patent on a showering system. Several companies currently manufacture equipment using this concept.

My interest in designing and developing this type of equipment has led to TV news coverage at both the local and international levels, and to a personal conversation with Dana Reeve, wife of Christopher Reeve. The same interest spawned financial support from Mr. George Mitchell, previous C.E.O of Mitchell Energy Company. His funding was used to build a robotic arm for the severely physically disabled. I have hopes of getting N.A.S.A. involved in this project, so that some day it can be brought into the marketplace. As finances allow, I continue to work on prototypes of equipment that will ultimately benefit this same population.

People have frequently asked what motivates me, and have told me that I am an inspiration to them. Here are some of my philosophies.

In my mind, motivation is composed primarily of energy, especially spiritual energy. Even the word "inspiration" can be loosely interpreted to mean "in spirit." In my mind, the root of spiritual energy is faith. The power (energy) of faith manifests itself in many forms. Some of these forms consist of a positive mental attitude, courage, patience, adaptability, and perseverance. It would be impossible to have a positive mental attitude if you didn't have faith that things would work out for the best in the end. People display courage because they have faith that the eventual outcome will be favorable. Faith permits us to have patience when things don't operate according to our timetables. Faith gives us the energy to persevere when the going gets tough. Faith also gives us the power to adapt or to seek other solutions to problems that beset us. I believe we all have access to the power of spiritual energy if we apply our faith. Historically, people's faith – and the energy that comes out of this faith – have had more to do with people's behavior, and hence the course of human events, than any other factor in existence. Just as animals and insects are born with instinctive powers unexplainable by science, mankind is also born with spiritual energy that is a gift from God. There are countless examples of how peoples' spiritual energy has enabled them to survive in the worst of circumstances.

Although my parents, wife, relatives, other role models, and my experiences have played an integral role in developing my faith and spiritual strength, I feel all have been orchestrated by God. The force of God deserves the most credit for my motivation. May that same force – God's spiritual energy – be with you.

~ Rick Myers

Rick, alongside just a few of his innovations
Photo by Bob Grace

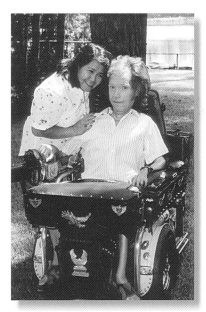

With his beloved wife, Teresita
Photo by Bob Grace

Meghan Rafferty
Photo by Picturemeportrait Studios

Cindy Cline-Flores

Everything For A Reason

The year 2005 was one of wonder for me: a time of ambitions, of dreams realized, and a clear harbinger of an exciting future. Fresh from graduating from my Emergency Medical Technician training, I landed a great job doing work that I loved with a major corporation, and was making enough money that I could actually see myself realizing my goal of owning my own home. Particularly in light of the fact that I lived in San Diego, a city known for its relatively high cost of living, this was no small feat. Yet even amidst all the successes I was experiencing, there remained an empty place inside me. It wasn't something I could really define. I just knew there was something I needed, some void in my life that longed to be filled. I was doing so much, yet even after working for three years as an EMT, I sensed in my core that I needed to be doing something more, something meaningful that had nothing to do with my own success.

For some months, I considered what this yearning might be. I thought long and hard about my options, about the things that filled my hours and my days, yet left my soul hungry. I prayed often for some sign, some guidance that would answer these vague questions that danced in the corners of my mind. This is the story of how those prayers were answered, and how, as is so often the case with answered prayers, the answers led me to even greater questions – and, ultimately, even greater answers.

As it turned out, I was far from alone in my desire to do something more. I spent a lot of time searching on the Internet, looking for some kind of organization or group that is called out to perform search and rescue type operations. I eventually found an article about a group of medical professionals called DMAT CA-4, that had been deployed to Guam in 2002 to help residents deal with the aftermath of a super typhoon. I did a Google search to learn more about the group, and eventually found their website. The site described the National Disaster Medical Systems (NDMS), a part of the Department of Health and Human Services, Office of Preparedness and Response. This federal system provides first-responder assistance for large-scale disasters, and is composed of volunteer civilian professionals who agree to be mobilized quickly to provide medical, psychological, and administrative support as part of the government response teams. The idea of being able to help people who were injured or displaced as a result of some cataclysmic event seemed to be exactly what I had been longing for, and I immediately went about the business of signing on as a member of a Disaster Medical Assistance Team (DMAT).

Most of the time, the team actively recruits members, rather than seeking applications from interested parties, so I probably didn't sit very high on their list at first. I was determined, however, and used every networking tool I could think of to get them interested in me. I didn't take their initial hesitance personally, because I figured they did things the way they did in order to ensure that the people on their teams are the right ones for the job. As an EMT, I understood the need for having people with not only the right qualifications, but the right kind of character and personality, to deal with the unique pressure and circumstances that are such a significant part of any rescue operation. Luckily for me, the response system is a pretty small and close-knit community, and my name was starting to make its way through the ranks as a young and energetic professional who really wanted to help. A few phone calls were made about me, and I was eventually given an application.

The process of coming on board was very intensive. The federal background check was nothing short of a review of my whole life story. They researched not only my entire history, but asked me questions such as what crimes I had committed but for which I had been neither caught nor convicted, and what would I have been charged with if I had been caught. What is a twenty-one-year-old supposed to say to questions like that? I guess I am a plain Jane, since I had never even tried illegal drugs, and was of legal drinking age, but wasn't big on drinking. In the end, I was left to put down that I had been caught speeding, and had paid a fine for a moving violation. They also wanted me to go back to my elementary school days and name someone who still knew me. They wanted information about all my past relationships, and a list of my exes. Great! I was not particularly excited to know what my old boyfriends would say about me. I even submitted to a credit check. It seemed that the system wanted to know how many time I had blown my nose in the last seven years (not really, but it sure felt like it!). After I had been put through that extensive vetting wringer, I had to be federally fingerprinted and photographed and entered into a federal database. The whole process took four months before I was accepted and made an active member of the team. I later discovered that my vetting was quicker than most, and that the process normally takes from six to eight months.

I understood the reason for such thoroughness, or thought I did. After all, each team is supplied and entrusted with enough drugs to kill three small countries. I figured that they had to make sure we were worthy of that trust, and that we were the best of the best. What I didn't know – but would learn only too soon – was that they were just as concerned with team members being up to the task of dealing with unbelievable pressures, in situations they had never even imagined, much less experienced.

I frequently get asked what a DMAT is, and I usually explain that it's like a MASH unit from the old television show, but operating in the United States, rather than in some war zone in another country. We set up operations not in hospitals, but in makeshift facilities in close proximity to the event, providing emergency triage and medical treatment and evacuation support. The teams are made up of volunteers who are all medical and auxiliary professionals in their "day jobs," yet who voluntarily take time away from their jobs to deploy to crisis zones as needed.

I jumped at the chance to be a part of such an elite group, attending any and all meetings and training sessions, and volunteering to help wherever it was needed. I wanted the DMAT administrators to see the eagerness and energy I could provide as an EMT for this team. Once I had jumped through all the requisite hoops and was accepted as a member of this effort, it seemed to me that the questions that had been nagging at me had finally been answered, and I was honestly high on life. I had the job I loved, belonged to something I knew was important, and I was getting closer to realizing my goal of owning a home with every paycheck! At long last, my life felt complete.

Then one Friday morning, my "day-job" boss sat me down and informed me that I had been doing a great job, so good in fact that I had accomplished their two-year goals in nine months, and had thus worked myself out of a job. To say that I never saw that one coming is a real understatement. This was the first time in my life that I had been let go from a job, and I was devastated. All my careful planning and efforts seemed at that moment to have been for naught. There was nothing to do but go home and start sending out my resume and pray that things really do happen for a reason, as so many people like to say when life deals them a bad hand. And believe me, I did pray.

After exactly two weeks to the day had passed, my faith in the declaration that things happen for a reason – as well as my faith in God – flickered brightly as the result of my getting a pre-recorded phone call, of all things. The recording said, "This is an activation notice of DMAT CA-4. You are currently listed on the roster as being available for 14 days. Please contact Zona (our administrative officer) for your deployment itinerary." As I listened to the message, my heart began pounding. I could feel the goose bumps rising on my flesh as adrenaline flooded my body. It was late August of 2005. Hurricane Katrina was coming, and I was going to be there to help.

When I contacted Zona, she asked if I would be able to not only deploy as an EMT but also as part of the Logistics group, and I immediately blurted out, "Yes!" Zona informed me that I would be contacted with further details of my deployment, and then she thanked me and hung up. I was literally in a daze, unsure, yet excited about what lay before me. I didn't get to enjoy that daze for very long, however. About five minutes after hanging up, I got a call from Terese, one of the doctors who happened to be the deputy commander of our team. She asked me if I still held a valid ambulance driver's license, and I told her that I did indeed have a current license.

"Well, how do you feel about driving a twenty-three-foot box truck from San Diego to New Orleans? It's just like driving an ambulance."

I was thinking, "No, it's not! When was the last time she drove either?" We had three of these trucks, which held everything that would be needed to set up a field hospital, from generators, to oral airways and other medical and surgical supplies, to water, and even our sleeping bags. No, this wouldn't be the same as driving an ambulance, but I didn't care. I was ready!

"Yes, of course!" I said without thinking much more about it. I was so afraid that if I said no, I would miss my chance and be passed over for deployment. Knowing that I was such a new member of the team, as well as one of the youngest, I recognized that this was a way to prove myself. This was a test I knew I could pass.

Then Terese added, "Well, how do you feel about being the only female to drive with five men?"

I didn't even need to think about that. We were all medical professionals, there for the same reason, and had all gone through a very thorough background check. "No problem," I replied.

"Great! Can you be here in forty-five minutes, fully packed and ready to roll?"

Forty-five minutes? Wow! I knew the call-out would be quick, but this was crazy. A normal call-out for our team was at least four hours, but I had to be there, and to show them just how much I wanted to be there, so I said yes.

I was pretty much packed and ready, just in case, but there was one phone call that I had to make, and I knew it was going to be difficult: I needed to call my mom. I am sure that getting a call from her twenty-one-year old daughter in the middle of her work day, saying I would be leaving in forty-five minutes to rush into the aftermath of a hurricane, was not what she had in mind for her day. Actually, though, I think that she was so caught up in her work when I called that she didn't know whether to cry, get excited, or just laugh. All she could do was tell me good luck, that she loved me, and to be safe. She understood why I felt called to be on this team, and knew that it was a big step for me.

Cindy Cline-Flores

I was partnered up with a very intelligent man from the Logistics group named Ed, a computer expert whose job was to help with the satellite phones and computers. His wife, an RN, was also deploying with the other forty-five members of our group who would be meeting on the LSU campus in Baton Rouge.

For the next three days, the five other drivers and I drove pretty much nonstop, stopping only to handle a multi-truck breakdown, to refuel, and to sleep in four-hour stints. Besides Ed and myself, the other drivers were Dave (the logistics chief), Kevin (an RN), Michael (a pharmacist), and Guy (a logistics specialist). We knew that time was of the essence, and we wanted to meet up with the rest of our team, which was flying ahead to LSU, as soon as possible.

Over the course of the long road trip, we got to know each other pretty well, as usually happens when people are confined in a vehicle for an extended period, and became a tight unit in the process. We called it our "bonding time," filled with jokes and shared stories of our lives and past deployments, readying ourselves for what might lay before us. This time was very special to me. I had never been east of Las Vegas before, and I felt very fortunate to share the experience with such a knowledgeable group of people, who were teaching me the ropes of DMAT life, and of life itself.

Late at night, while driving through the middle of nowhere in New Mexico, Guy radioed my truck and asked, "Meggs, what do you think of New Mexico?"

I replied with an enthusiastic, "It's beautiful!"

Immediately, everybody broke out in laughter. The truth is, it was so dark that we couldn't see a thing beyond the narrow patch illuminated by our headlights. But it was beautiful to me; the pure white stars against a deep black and cloudless sky, coupled with the excitement of this unknown adventure, made it very easy for me to pray in a way that I had not done in a long time. This time, instead of being merely a plea for divine help or protection, my prayer was an expression of profound gratitude and wonder. It was easy to see God's abundant beauty in everything, even set within the blackness of the desert night.

The storm hit New Orleans and the levees failed while we were driving somewhere in Texas, but the information our team was receiving was sketchy, at best. We had no idea as to the extent of the damage, nor the number of people injured. We arrived at our rendezvous point at LSU, only to find that our team had been sent ahead into New Orleans with another team. This was not going over too well with any of us, and when we were told that we were going somewhere else rather than to join up with the rest of our team, that was the last straw for Dave. He persuaded the team coordinators to let us go meet up with our own team, and we left quickly, before they could change their minds. As we hurried to meet our team, the profound scope of

Mother Nature's power became more and more evident. The light-hearted banter between the trucks stopped, and we all fell silent. Both sides of the highway into New Orleans were jammed with cars headed out of town, barely moving. Our convoy was on the emergency lane, headed in.

Once we arrived in the city, I was struck by an image I hadn't expected at all. It reminded me of a ghost town. It was two in the morning when we reached the Louis Armstrong Airport, and the scene there is best described as bedlam, though I would imagine that bedlam would seem organized in comparison.

There was no power, no airport personnel, and even more surprising, no planes. We quickly set up our treatment tents in an area under a skylight, so we would be able to use natural light as much as possible. The generators that we had brought would be needed to power the lights inside the tents and all of our medical equipment, but there was no way they could provide enough power to light up the entire area.

We were all exhausted, but there was already a line of people waiting – some in need of medical attention, and many others waiting for a plane to take them away, anywhere but here. Unfortunately, it would be days before any of these people would be moved out, and even longer for those who weren't in need of further medical treatment. We kept asking ourselves how these people knew to come here, of all places, for medical care.

We were getting thousands and thousands of people from all walks of life, from nursing homes, hospitals, psychiatric wards, methadone clinics, and more young adolescents in need of dialysis than I have ever seen in my life. We also started seeing more and more people who were taken off of rooftops and rescued from parks, as well as many who had waded through miles of waist-deep and even chest-deep water, seeking a place of safety.

It had been over twenty-four hours since we had arrived on-site, and a lot of driving before that since I had slept. I was deliriously tired, but so much had to be done, and I simply did not have the heart to tell someone in need that I needed sleep, and that someone else would have to help them. So I kept going until one of the team leaders saw how punchy I was getting, and ordered me to go sleep for a few hours.

Most of our team slept on the baggage carousel (since there was no power, it was not moving). I was pulled to one of our trucks with one of our RNs and told to sleep in the back. While the back of a cargo truck might not seem like the best place to sleep, it was dark, safe (or at least safer than an open area), and since it was a refrigerated truck, it was probably the only place in the airport that wasn't stiflingly hot. Compared to everywhere else, it actually felt nice. Dave, my logistics chief, slept in the

Cindy Cline-Flores

front of the truck. It made me feel a lot safer being tucked away like that, knowing that if the situation deteriorated to the point where we were in physical danger, all Dave had to do was drive away and we would be out of it.

After a few hours of sleep, I awakened to even more of a war zone than what I had left only hours before. Helicopters of all shapes and sizes – military, Coast Guard, and private – were making hot drops of people in two lines, with at least twelve helos landing and taking off every three minutes, round the clock, and up to sixteen in the air at any given time. This was a process that I never got used to seeing. Out in front of the airport, there was a massive procession of ambulances, four abreast and over forty-five deep, unmoving, waiting in queue to unload their wounded passengers. As they inched their way up, they would unload like the clown cars you see in the movies, with more people emerging from the box-like vehicles than you would think capable of fitting into such a small vehicle. It got so bad at one point that ambulances were running out of fuel as they idled, waiting to pull up.

This was the largest mass triage situation that any of us had ever seen or even heard about. We had a red tent where they brought the "oh my, they are gonna die" patients, a yellow tent for the "urgent but not emergent" patients, and a green tent that was for the walking wounded. Within minutes of being set up, however, the green tent was converted into another yellow tent, so great was the overflow of injured people. There was also a "black tag" area, set apart from the others, specifically for patients who were under hospice care or had "do not resuscitate" orders. Efforts in the black tag area were limited to making the patients as comfortable as possible. There were two wonderful teammates in our logistics group who served as both psychiatrist and chaplain in this most critical area, and I will never forget their compassion, their gentleness, and their strength. I know that the sheer magnitude of human suffering we observed, as well as the unimaginable amount of death, had a profound effect upon all of us, but I think that it affected these two – and those who worked alongside them – even more than it did the rest of us. Merely observing such a large-scale triage touched us all in a way I simply cannot describe, but actually participating – and deciding who was well enough to receive the limited amount of care we could provide, versus those who were beyond our help, and would be left to die – is an experience that will haunt me for the rest of my life.

As you might imagine (but I honestly hope you cannot), my days there seemed to all run together in one long blur. There was no real way to keep track, or even any reason to do so. We were there to do a job, and that's all that mattered. At one point, there was a locomotive engine lifted by four of the hugest military helicopters I'd ever seen and put on the tarmac of the airport. Its massive generator, which normally provided power to its gigantic electric wheel motors, was hooked up to the airport's power grid, and we were able to get the airport's power up to about twenty percent. It doesn't sound like much, but it made a big difference. Once it was in operation, we got a few lights, and flushing automatic toilets, which were a vast improvement over the non-functioning toilets that had long since been overwhelmed by the sheer number of people using them.

One unfortunate result of the lack of power and the masses of people was that they would relieve themselves and vomit wherever they were. Some were afraid to move out of fear of losing their place in line or being separated from their loved ones, while others were simply unable to get up off the ground. Add the smell of throngs of people who had slogged through unimaginable filth without access to the means to tend to their personal hygiene, coupled with the oppressively high heat and humidity, and the resulting stench permeated everything, and will probably stay in my nose – or at least my memory – forever.

I saw some of the most horrific things happen to people there, in that time of desperation and crisis. I saw women and children raped, people shot, mothers not caring for their newborns, and most disturbing, acts of unthinkable violence perpetuated against us, the very people who were trying to help them. I was the target of one such attack, as were so many others who had come here of their own accord just to alleviate these people's suffering. When it happened, I have to admit that I was numbed to the horror of the experience. It just didn't seem real to me. How could it be?

I was there for three days before I cried. It was so overwhelming – so much to take in, and so surreal. In my mind, I knew that this couldn't be happening. There was no way that such selflessness could exist in the same place with such evil. All I knew was how to swallow it, be strong, and keep moving. When I finally did cry, it felt good. It was only when I allowed myself the comfort and release of tears that the world in which I found myself became real. The hurt, the pain, the filth and smell, and the ever-present danger… it was all really happening.

We were running out of supplies left and right, and we were finding new uses for things all the time. I used to laugh at the way military people would jerry-rig things in the movies when they lacked a piece of needed equipment, but I quickly learned that their kind of inventiveness was very real, and often very necessary. To this day, duct tape is something that I take with me everywhere I go!

We had just received a hundred wool blankets from the Army, and they were all neatly stacked inside in our logistics area. An elderly woman happened to see them, and came up to me and asked how much a blanket would cost. She quickly added that it was not for her, but for her husband, pointing to where he lay on the ground about a hundred yards away. He was one of about three hundred people from the same nursing home, all laid out in rows on the ground. My heart jumped in my throat at the sight. I swallowed hard, smiled at her, and told her that they didn't cost anything. I told her that I was glad to have just gotten them, so I would be able to give her one.

She corrected me. "Not for me. For my husband."

I handed it to her and saw the fear and loneliness in her eyes, and she returned to her husband's side. Not three minutes later, she came back to me with the blanket. "If you would lend me your scissors, and if it is ok, I will cut this blanket in half. It is large, and if I cut it in half, I will be able to cover the man lying next to my husband, too."

All I could do was cry and help her cut the blanket. What a selfless woman. Through all of this, she was still thinking of how she could help others. Not only her ailing husband, but a complete stranger next to him, as well. I watched her walk back to her husband's side, knowing that I had just met the strongest woman in the world. To this day, talking about the woman and the blanket brings me to tears.

At another point, we had two women come off of a helicopter with four babies each in their arms. They were RNs from a local hospital. The nurses' arms were banded to match the bands the newborns wore. When we asked them where the infants came from, they looked at us with hopelessness in their eyes. "These are the newborns that were left. Their mothers left without them." In the few hours that the nurses and the newborns were there, they told me bits of their stories. They told me of sending their own families and young children ahead days earlier, so they could bear the storm and take care of the others who were left behind.

These women are my heroes; to take on the responsibility of not one but eight abandoned newborns in a disaster zone is a brave and wonderful thing.

We saw a lot of women with their own newborn babies who were suffering the effects of severe dehydration and stress, and were not doing well. I had to bite my tongue to keep from spewing the rage I felt toward these women. They didn't have a bottle or diapers, let alone food for their babies, and were unable to tell us the last time the infants had voided or eaten. But they had more looted bags – mostly of luxury items and booze – than I had ever seen. I never understood this type of selfishness, and I'm not proud of feeling so angry at them. I am, however, proud of the fact that of all of the infants we saw, we did not lose a single one. We delivered nine babies at the airport, and airlifted our midwife, who successfully delivered breach twins on the way to Houston.

There was another woman who appeared from somewhere out of the masses, who did not need medical attention. She came up and said, "I see that trash and stuff is getting high all over. If you let me borrow a pair of gloves, I'll find a place for it and help." You better believe that we gave her all the gloves she wanted. A willing helping hand with things like that gave us more time to treat people. After a while, she was helping to turn people who were on litters and couldn't move themselves, which helped reduce the chance that they would get bed sores, and prevented the sores they did have from growing worse. She was quite a busy bee, with a smile on her face – even singing at times – and always there to help us with anything we needed. In talking with her here and there, I found out that she had lost everything in the hurricane, and had nothing left but the clothes on her back to show for her life thus far. And yet, she wanted only to give…

One of the first patient planes that went out had a seat for her on it, but she looked at us and said, "Where would I go? I have nothing. Give my spot to someone who really needs it. I can do more good here, and I have more to give." There were no words that any of us could say that would do justice to what we felt for this remarkable woman. There were hugs and tear-filled eyes all around, then we all went back to work. She had such a wonderful attitude and a deep faith in God, in a time and place where my own faith was being so deeply challenged. She was rich in her faith and knew her calling.

Very soon after we got set up in the airport, a group of Air Marshals came up to us in the logistics area. One came to me and said he was a paramedic and was here to help get these people out of the airport and on planes, but they were finding a lot of minor medical issues that he could fix before moving them out. He needed to know what forms and such he needed to fill out, and Dave and I laughed at the idea. We were all on the same team here, and we gladly gave him anything that we had that he needed. At least once a day, the Air Marshal came up and re-stocked with me. We talked and started to get to know one another. He knew a lot about San Diego, having spent time there in his youth, and we both welcomed the opportunity to talk about something completely apart from the death and suffering all around us.

About a week had passed, and the medical patients had been flown out to hospitals, and most of the evacuees had been flown out to various evacuee centers around the country. Things had slowed down dramatically for us, and we knew it was time to hand this operation over to a fresh team. Our wonderful helper who had cleaned and aided so many people finally took a seat on a plane to go to her sister's, and we were happy to know she had a place to go. My Air Marshal friend asked for my information, saying he wanted to write my employer and tell them how thankful he was that I was able to be there. When I told him that I had been laid off two weeks before, he laughed, and said he would write a letter of recommendation instead.

We left the airport in a mad dash through a very unsafe city, escorted by police cruisers with lights and sirens blaring, until we were almost in Baton Rouge. I felt what it was like to be a dignitary, albeit one who was hated and being shot at! We spent the night hidden at the Louisiana School for the Deaf, where the people welcomed us to their basketball court floor and made us a wonderful hot meal. I was in hog heaven, being fluent in sign language. We left early the following day, after a hot shower and hot coffee, driving on to Houston, Texas. From there we would fly home.

Sitting at the airport in Houston was so weird. Televisions were blaring news coverage of Katrina, but we were actually surrounded by people who didn't need anything from us. We were excited to see what the news people were saying, thinking we might even see some coverage of our efforts. But instead, there was story after story about how nobody was helping, and how the government had failed; there were even accusations that we had been euthanizing people! The group started to console one another. We knew what we had seen and done, but we weren't coming home heroes in the media's eyes.

Home at last! I think I took the longest shower of my life that first day back, and then a long, leisurely bath, but I still didn't feel clean. I still could smell the filth and the death. I managed to do most of my laundry before my mother came home, because I didn't want her to be nauseated by the smell that lingered on everything I had. I told her not to touch my boots or other things until I could get rid of them or disinfect them. She was a little shocked, but was happy just to have me home.

It took me about another week to get back into the swing of things. I was still a bit weird about seeing people in restaurants wasting food and drinks, feeling they should be thankful and finish what they had ordered. My mother saw a difference in me, too. She took me shopping shortly after I got back, knowing that getting me outside was a good thing. She asked me why I kept looking at the floor, instead of talking to people and looking at things as I had always done. I told her that I didn't mean to, it was just that I didn't want people to ask me anything, or to ask anything of me. It was a defense mechanism we had learned at the airport, where we had to step over twenty people to help one. We would be stopped at every turn by someone who needed our help – or at least, our attention – and we quickly learned that if we heeded every plea that was directed at us, we might never get to the one person whom we had started out to help. Plus, the weight of that massive triage experience made me want to be as far removed from being responsible for someone else's life-or-death situation as I could get.

By the time the second week rolled around, I had gotten a few job offers and gladly took one. The Air Marshal and I kept in touch by e-mail, and he assumed the role of my mentor. It was only a few months before he was able to come out and enjoy a California vacation. My family was glad to meet him, and thankful that there had been people looking out for me there. I was glad that I not only had my team, but someone with whom I could talk about anything that had happened there, and who would understand. I couldn't tell my family everything, as they would be fearful of my ever deploying again.

I did go through several decompression sessions with my team, where we discussed how we were doing back in the "real world," and how we were adjusting. Some were doing better than others, but I was relieved to learn that what I was feeling was normal. The team administrators advised us to not change anything significant in our lives for six months – don't get married, don't get divorced, don't buy or sell a house, no new pets or children. They didn't want us to make snap choices that might be influenced by post-traumatic stress syndrome, and which we might ultimately come to regret. The team and I share a bond far stronger than any I have ever known. They became my family.

Early in the following spring, I went out to Texas to visit the Air Marshal and fell in love! Not with him, but with Texas. In all of the changes I was going through after my experiences in New Orleans, I had began to realize how much I didn't enjoy San Diego any more. The people there were different now; perhaps it was me who came home different, but they all seemed fake, trendy, superficial, and cold. The culture in Texas was poles apart from what I had known in San Diego. The people here – like the weather – were so warm, and they felt so down-to-earth and real. Strangers were actually kind to one another. I didn't want to go home after that visit, but I knew I had to. Deep down, though, I knew I would be back!

Six months and twenty-six days later, I packed up my truck and moved to my first apartment in the Dallas/Fort Worth area. I had lined up a job here, and had my Air Marshal mentor take a look at the apartment before I moved to make sure I was in a place that he could give my mother the safety nod to. Things happened so fast once I moved. I found my faith in people again. Even though I had seen some of the worst people in the world, there were great people too, and the wonderful people I had encountered made more of an impact on me than had the bad ones. I had gone down to New Orleans to help others, but I ended up learning (and, my mom would say, growing) more than I could have ever expected. It gave me the strength to move on my own to a different state where I knew only one person, and then to buy a home of my own, as I had dreamed of doing. I could actually afford a home here in Texas, whereas I would have had to work and save a lot longer to afford one in California. And a perfect home it is, too: my safe haven. I had completed my original goal, and achieved other goals I hadn't even considered.

Shortly after I moved into my home, when I wasn't even looking for a relationship, I was set up on a blind date, and I found a soul mate that night. I guess it is true that love finds you when you're not looking. We married, and for a time, it seemed like what we had would be one of those "happily ever after" tales we dreamt about as children. While he was truly the man of my dreams, I have had to realize that dreams – like people – change, and we began to grow apart. That the marriage didn't last might once have felt like yet another failure, but I have come to recognize that it has played a significant role in my own growth, and (I like to think) in the life of the man I wed. I am happy to say that now, four years after Katrina, while I am no longer married to the man of my dreams, I am in a place of renewed and strengthened faith in God, as well as the many good people in my life. My mother, sister, co-workers and friends are more precious to me than I could ever express. I continue to deploy with my DMAT CA-4 family, and I still have one great mentor, as well! None of this would have happened if I had not been willing to drive a big truck and hang out with the guys on a trip down to New Orleans. No one can tell me that things don't happen for a reason. I know they do!

The vague yearning that defined my life before I went to New Orleans has given way to a clarity of purpose seasoned by pain and doubt, yet possessed of a richness I had never imagined possible. Having come face to face with the ugliest side of human nature and the most desperate kind of suffering imaginable, I also have been touched by the absolute best of humanity, and have been blessed by a joy that no amount of suffering can overwhelm. The face of that ugliness and suffering will linger in my memory for the rest of my life, yet so will the beauty and joy I found. In the end, I know that no matter how deep the despair one might feel, there is always hope.

~ *Meghan Rafferty*

Alden and Travis Clark
Photo by Alisa Murray

Cindy Cline-Flores

Behold!
A Son

Whatever you ask for in prayer, believe that you have received it, and it will be yours. Mark 11:24

A few years ago, this Bible passage would have meant very little to me. Now it is my mantra that I've condensed to "believe." I have grown to know that "believe" is the most powerful word in existence. It is even more powerful than the word "love," for only after we believe in love can we find it. This is the story of how I came to believe in love.

There is one thing I have always wanted to be: a dad. When I decided to make that dream a reality I sought some advice from my church minister, Karen Tudor. "How do I, a single man, have a baby?" I asked.

Karen told me I already had. "When you give birth to an idea in your heart and believe in it," she said, "it will find you." I began to pray for my son to come into my life.

Within weeks of that affirmation I received a phone call from a friend. He wanted to introduce me to a pregnant woman he knew. Excited, I quickly agreed to meet her.

As we exited the freeway, he said, "We're here." We parked on the corner, not near any building, and I looked around, confused. Then I saw her, a pregnant woman, panhandling on the corner. After my friend introduced us, she and I walked to her box community in the woods. What had I gotten myself into?

I offered to get her the medical help she needed. She accepted, but declared that she would not leave the woods, for this was her home and her community. Over the course of weeks I tried to find a doctor who would see a pregnant homeless woman. After a few hundred attempts, we found a doctor at Baylor Medical School who agreed to see her as a case study for his students.

Initially we visited the doctor three times in one week. The first visit confirmed that she was about five months pregnant, though she had no clue when she might have conceived. It also revealed she was epileptic and often suffered from seizures, which was not good for her or the baby. On the second visit she revealed the history of her life on the streets. Hers was a long history of drug abuse from crack, cocaine, alcohol or whatever she could score that day, along with chain smoking and sleeping on the ground in a tent. The third visit brought the most disturbing news of all: she had a severe case of syphilis.

The following week I sat with the doctor, who handed me stacks of information on pregnancy and all the complications the fetus might already have suffered. The seizures alone might have already caused severe damage. The drugs would have rotted the fetus' brain and body, and the syphilis would have wiped out any hope of this child ever living. The doctor scheduled a sonogram for the next week.

Each day I drove to the woods to deliver dinner and all the comforts I could provide, but the woman still refused to leave. At the next doctor's visit, the sonogram revealed that she was carrying a girl. What a relief, I sighed, for I knew in my heart I was having a boy. This was not my son. The girl was still too small for the doctor to tell how much damage it had already suffered.

I talked to the mom and told her I would continue to support her through the rest of the pregnancy, and even help her find placement for this girl. She had no desire to keep this child or change her life in any way.

At seven months I convinced the woman to move into a hotel and sleep in a bed. She reluctantly agreed and moved into a hotel near my house. Doctor visits became regular and she gained weight and started taking better care of herself.

The doctor informed us that he could get a good sonogram around the eighth month that would tell him what parts of the fetus had or hadn't developed. He forewarned us that we might see a fetus with no legs or arms, a head with no eye sockets or nose, or something even worse than we could imagine. As he began the sonogram, however, he was pleased that he could see four proportional limbs and two eyes, and that the rest of the head and torso all seemed in proportion as well.

At that moment the room became perfectly still and quiet. It filled with a bright white light. Peace washed over everything. At that moment the baby turned for all of us to see. A voice washed over my spirit that said, "Your faith has made you well."

The next voice was the doctor's. "It seems someone decided to grow a little something extra. We have a boy." And I had a son.

As delivery time approached the doctor warned us what to expect. "Although things appeared proportional on the sonogram," he said, "this child cannot be born healthy." I believed different.

Travis was born at 3:00 in the morning. As he entered the world, the doctor and nurses were prepared for the worst. They'd brought in lots of emergency equipment to combat whatever birth defect they'd face upon my son's arrival. I brought with me faith and a prayer team.

When Travis arrived the nurse said, "No way."

The doctor said, "It's not possible."

I said, "What do you expect from God?"

Travis stayed in the hospital for three days as the medical staff studied, poked, and needled him, looking for birth defects. At the end of the third day they handed me my "perfect" son. The doctor said, "I really can't believe my eyes. I've never seen such a beautiful baby."

As I write this, Travis is four years old. And he's more than just healthy; he's a vibrant, lively child. The bright light still trails everywhere he goes.

Do miracles really exist in the 21st century? I guess my question would be: Do you believe in miracles?

~ *Alden Clark*

Barbara Snitkin
Photo by Alisa Murray

Cindy Cline-Flores

Disguised Blessing

This great adventure that is my life began when I was born a Navy brat in Pensacola, Florida. Like other children of career military members, my childhood was spent bouncing around from base to base, living in Seattle, Washington, San Diego, California, Cocoa Beach, Florida, and Tacoma, Washington. Moving from place to place was an educational opportunity in itself. My dad taught me to fly when I was twelve years old. I loved practicing stalls in the Aeronica Champion. With dad in the back seat talking to me right over my shoulder, I knew without a doubt I could do anything he talked me through. Young Navy boys were scratching their heads when I executed a perfect three-point landing and taxied up to the hangar; they couldn't understand how a twelve-year-old girl could do that so well. I knew in my heart it was because I had complete faith in my dad and what he told me I could do!

After my dad retired from the Navy, we moved to the company town of Newgulf, Texas, where he and a friend owned a small airport, and Dad worked as the corporate pilot for Texas Gulf Sulphur. Newgulf was a unique community, and it was great fun moving there as a freshman in high school, and getting all the attention that comes with being the new girl in town.

Then, the week before I was to leave for college, I was in a terrible accident, just one month after another car accident had killed three of my classmates, devastating our little town. I had been riding on the hood of a tractor when the front wheel hit a deep hole, bouncing me off backwards and allowing the big back wheel to roll over me. As I lay there, my boyfriend, Ronnie, was kneeling beside me on my left, so scared. In that moment, I saw another boy, David, who had been killed in the earlier accident, standing just to my right. I remember that he was wearing his usual Levi's and a white cowboy shirt, and I could see his FFA belt buckle gleaming in the sunlight. He extended his hand to me, as if to have me come with him. I was so peaceful, and the space and light were so beautiful, that I was tempted to reach for his hand and go with him. Then I turned to Ronnie and said, "I don't want to die." In that instant, David just disappeared. I knew then that I was going to be just fine. It was much later that I realized that I had gone through a near-death experience. I can honestly say that it was easily the most peaceful, beautiful experience I've ever had, and one that forever changed the way I looked at my life and the universe around me.

Though I was critically injured, and spent three months in the hospital, I was able to console my mom and dad, assuring them that I would be okay. The time I spent in the hospital, and my experiences with the professionals who cared for me, inspired me to go on to college and eventually become a nurse. I loved my career, and my insider's view of the patient's perspective made me very good at my work.

In 1995, my thirty-two-year marriage ended in divorce, and three months later, I was diagnosed with leukemia. This was startling news, but somehow in that moment, it actually made a lot of sense to me. I had been living my life in such conflict and turmoil in the marriage that everything was out of balance, which had to include my immune system. I saw this as dis-ease, rather than disease. Some people might see the difference between the two as insignificant, but I knew better. With this realization, I had moved from three years of turmoil while trying to manage a divorce to a space of real freedom. I knew that I could follow my instincts and be with what my heart told me. I was perfect, whole, and complete in God's eyes, and I felt the comfort of peace. I truly was able to look at all my options and come from the sense that I would be guided in my recovery. People from my past were suddenly showing up, and I was not hesitant in sharing my situation. One of those friends put together an e-mail network of my friends and family, to keep everyone informed on my status. I had prayer and meditation going on all the time. I used my newly-learned Chi Gong, visualization, and meditation time, and began a rigorous nutrition program.

The doctors were dismayed at the aggressiveness of my leukemia. After undergoing six chemotherapy treatments, there was no turn for the better. The oncologist told me my case was a nasty one, and that the outlook was grim. He told me I needed a bone marrow transplant, and that it would be the only thing that could save my life. He went on to tell me that they had no survival statistics for a transplant patient in my age group, and that I could die in the first four weeks after the transplant. Even with the risks, they insisted I had to undergo the procedure if I were to have any chance of survival. My name was put in the National Bone Marrow Registry to try to match me up with an acceptable donor. I continued researching the options on my own, even though I was in the hospital every 10 days or so for blood transfusions. I just couldn't produce enough red blood cells to keep me going.

I knew in my heart that the dire predictions I was hearing weren't true. I talked with bone marrow transplant teams in other cities, and they all agreed with my oncologist's assessment of my case – and the poor prognosis I had been given. I held out because I felt I would be fine with the quality life I could expect in the short term, and I had no fear of death, if that was ultimately to be. My comfort came from my near-death experience as an eighteen-year-old, which had really deepened my spiritual awareness.

Cindy Cline-Flores

Suddenly, a new type of chemotherapy – so new that it had not even been written about in the medical journals – was offered to me. After only two of these treatments, my leukemia went into remission.

I now looked at life with a whole new view. Colors were more vivid, sunsets more beautiful, and flowers more abundant than ever before. I grew to love searching the night sky, looking for the Big Dipper and Venus. I really became present in my life and the universe, awed by how magical it all is. As I was becoming so filled with this newfound wonder, my son and his wife told me that they were pregnant with my first grandchild. One day, I got a call from my daughter-in-law, inviting me to come to their last class in preparation for childbirth. They wanted me to hear what the nurse had to say about the possibility of harvesting the stem cells of the newborn from the umbilical cord and having it stored for stem cell transplant. She told us that the stem cells could be used, not only by the newborn itself, but by another family member, as well. She went on to say that a stem cell transplant from the newborns' cord blood is safer than that from a bone marrow donor – even one who is a perfect match. This was great news, not only for me, but also for baby Lucas, because these stem cells could be preserved for him or his siblings, should the need ever arise. To say that we were excited about the possibilities would be a big understatement, and we eagerly signed up. The next thing we knew, ABC News contacted us, and came to my son's home to interview us as a family, since we were be one of the first to have this procedure done.

I remained in remission for six and a half years. I felt perfectly fine, living a full life and continuing to work in my job. Then, in 2003, the leukemia showed up again in my blood work. Of course, chemotherapy had improved, and I went through the six treatments with flying colors, knowing all along that this too would pass. The stem cell transplant was not needed. I am so clear that even these challenges are all part of my life's journey. Nothing wrong, just life as it shows up. I get to choose to live it and fulfill my greatest potential, even in the face of dis-ease.

Continuing on my exciting journey, I deepen my awareness of my spiritual path each day. My disguised blessing – leukemia – is the catalyst that has inspired me to be a stand-in, coaching others who find themselves facing a health challenge. I want to share a truth that has become so clear to me: that it is up to us to be in affirmative action into the inquiry and choices we make in living quality lives. And that we are perfect beings, whole and complete in God's eyes.

~ *Barbara Snitkin*

Billy and Linda Garrett
Photo by Alisa Murray

Cindy Cline-Flores

Full Circle

Ever since the third grade, Farmington, New Mexico in the Four Corners area had been my home. Then, in the summer between my junior and senior year in high school, my family moved to south Louisiana and, very soon thereafter, to West Texas. After lengthy discussions (and no small amount of pleading on my part), my parents consented to let me return to Farmington, where all my friends were, to live with the family of a long-time friend while I finished high school. About six weeks before graduation, I had a trampoline accident that left me paralyzed from the neck down.

A fine neurosurgeon in Albuquerque brought me through traction, cervical fusion, and double pneumonia before sending me to Denver, where I spent the next year in a rehabilitation facility. After I was discharged from the hospital, I returned to West Texas. In the year that I was there, I continued to recuperate with the care and comfort of a tough-minded, positive family who constantly encouraged me, but didn't coddle me. They helped me when I needed it, but cut me no slack if I tried to use my condition to get my way.

In the fall of 1967, we moved to Houston, where I began a degree program that, after a detour to a B.A., culminated in a Bachelor of Science degree. Shell Oil Company hired me as an information technology worker in 1974, and I have had the good fortune to continue my career with Shell to the present day.

Throughout all those years, my post-accident situation afforded me the opportunity (I can call it that today) to encounter numerous mental, physical, and social challenges and, thankfully, to overcome many of them. With loving help from family, friends, co-workers, and – at times – strangers, I was able to conquer many daily obstacles that most people never encounter, such as dressing myself, getting into and out of cars, negotiating curbs and stairs, and even recovering from the occasional embarrassment of having inadequate control of my bodily functions. I was eventually able to live by myself, drive myself, and take care of most of life's daily chores.

The afternoon of my accident, my high school girlfriend and first love was participating in an after-school meeting. When she left the meeting to meet me, she learned of the accident. That afternoon in the emergency room and a subsequent visit to Albuquerque were the last times we saw one another. Then, in the normal process of leaving high school years behind and making a life, we lost contact. Linda later married and raised two sons and a daughter.

Then in late 1999, I entered my name and contact information into an alumni web site. Soon after, Linda's youngest son happened to be browsing through the site, and came across my information. Chad was excited to share the discovery with his mother, knowing that Linda had tried to learn of my whereabouts and my progress over the years, so she could relay the news to her family. After Chad e-mailed me, I telephoned Linda, and we seemed to pick up right where we left off so many years earlier. She told me all about what had happened in her life in the intervening years, and about her three adult children, whom she obviously adored. One thing led to another, and in the fall of 2000, we married.

To anyone faced with a life-changing injury, I would offer these thoughts: We can never know in advance how things will work out, and what seems at the moment to be devastating will often improve over time. What is more, even if the situation itself fails to change, our perception of it almost surely will. We adapt. The important thing is to persevere and struggle against any negative thinking. I can honestly say (and I think my family, my friends, and my wife would agree) that my life has been and continues to be good, happy, and productive.

~ *Billy Garrett*

Christina Dharamsingh
Photo by Dzung Ky

Cindy Cline-Flores

Running Away To Home

I firmly believe that we as individuals have the power and the opportunity to strive and make our dreams a reality. I have learned that with courage, a successful woman can fail at some things, then learn from her failures powerful lessons to mold her future.

I was born in Trinidad, raised with strong Christian values by a Pentecostal preacher dad and a Sunday school teacher mom. I believe that the foundation for my faith was the prayers that were embedded in my soul from the age of three. I have always believed that my greatest gifts have been the freedom of prayer and the miracles achieved from the dedication I placed on God and his daily blessings. My mother, Kamal Bagaloo, is in her seventies, and a great prayer warrior. She prays almost constantly, for everything and everyone, so whenever I have a dilemma, I go to her for prayer.

My other source of spirituality came from my beloved friend, Sister Rose, who recently passed away. Rose prayed with me and for me for over 30 years. She never judged me, she just prayed. She was my rock and tower of strength, like my second mother. I call her my New York Mom. I was so blessed to have two spiritual moms who were there for me at all times, and whose love helped me build my faith. They always told me to continue to trust God in all things, and that He will never fail. I know that He is always there with me. Even when things are the gloomiest and we feel there is nowhere to turn, God will never leave us or forsake us, but will carry us through all our difficult times.

I was very fortunate to be given the opportunity to attend school in Trinidad, at a renowned convent named St. Charles Girls' High School. After five years, I had a burning desire to be a nun, and turn my life over to God and be a missionary. I wanted to go to India or Africa and help the homeless and hungry. I never wanted to get married and go through the hurt and pain I see so many women endure. My dream was crushed because I had to make a decision to either get married to a man whom I did not know and move to New York, or stay in my own country and face a hard life. I looked at the hardship my family was facing in my country, and thought about the opportunity I could offer them if I were to marry and move to the US. After much consideration, my parents decided to have me married.

I barely knew my husband. He had come down to visit and get engaged, and within two months I flew up to New York, where we were married. We were two entirely different people with very different religious backgrounds. I believed that if I just talked to him and prayed for him, he would accept God as his Savior, but I was wrong. He became worse, daily. My abuse began on January 31st, 1970, and did not end until November 30th, 1982. My husband did not talk much; our "conversations" usually were limited to him beating me to a pulp, until I was bloody, unconscious, and could not move. He was about 6 feet, 5 inches tall, and weighed approximately 180 pounds. I only weighed 84 pounds, so it was nothing for him to throw me to the floor and kick me and stomp all over me until I could not move. Even though this was happening in New York, my culture had taught me that this is what life was supposed to be, and that this was a wife's punishment. I felt I had no right to complain to him or anyone about the abuse. Also, divorce was not an option, because it is looked upon as a big disgrace by our society, especially by my family back home.

After many years of beatings, rape, torture and abuse, one day I could not take it any more. While I was cooking, he came into the kitchen to hit me and I raised the big spoon and hit him so hard on his forehead that it cut him. He was so shocked, he jumped back about six feet, totally stunned. Then I told him that I would kill him if he ever touched me again. I was so scared, because I knew in my heart that he would kill me that day. He almost did. I was beaten so badly that my face was flowing with blood, and he had punctured my spleen and broken some ribs. I ran away the first chance I had, and the police took me to the hospital. When I called my parents to beg them to let me return home, they tried to discourage me, and told me my place was with my husband. So I had to go back again, and the abuse continued. I could see no end to the suffering I faced, and once I actually tried to commit suicide. At the time, I did not ask God whether this was okay or not. I was so fed up and wanted my suffering to end. I knew life had to be better than hell, but mine was utter hell anyway, and I thought that at least hell was some other place, not here. My life even felt worse than before, because I felt that God would not forgive me. I begged God for forgiveness and tried to move on.

Two years into the marriage, I was blessed with a daughter, and knew I had to survive for her sake. Though I had previously attempted suicide, I now knew that it was not an option. I realized it was not the answer. But what were the answers? I could not see any way that my life could be better unless I left. However, I wondered how, without a better education, could I

Cindy Cline-Flores

support my daughter? One day, my friend Barbara Ramcharitar, who has been my positive mentor for many years, encouraged me to get my college degree in New York, so I could eventually leave this man.

She helped me with the application, and I started college at New York Community College and Long Island University. I completed an Associates Degree in Accounting and a Bachelors Degree in Science. I was working to get my MBA in Management, but knew I could not finish the masters degree program while still going through the abuse. I was working a full time job, going to college nights and weekends, maintaining a 21-credit course load, and caring for an infant child. At the same time, I was being beaten several times a week, both in the mornings and evenings, by my abusive husband. He was totally against me going to college, but I did not care at the time; I decided to take all the beatings if he would only allow me to finish college. I knew that in the end, I would succeed, and I did.

For thirteen years, college was my escape from the prison walls of my marriage. I studied harder. The more abuse I got, the harder I studied, because I knew one day I would be leaving with my daughter. By that time I was pregnant with my son. As soon as he was three months old, I left. I remember the last night in that house. My husband was an alcoholic and I guess a little mentally insane. He took me downstairs to the boiler room, stripped me naked, and tied me to the big boiler with a piece of rope. He had carefully sharpened a handful of knives, and laid them across the boiler. He began running the knives all over my body, describing in graphic detail how he would mutilate my body parts and feed them to me. At that moment, I closed my eyes and saw my death. He was grinding his teeth, standing tall over me, smelling of liquor. I was sure I was soon going to be dead. I prayed what I thought would be my last prayer. I was begging God to please take me away before he touched me. I had endured enough abuse for thirteen years. The torture had to stop; the rapes must stop; my life must end. Then there was silence. I opened my eyes, and he was gone.

I was too scared to move. I thought he was behind me, waiting to strike me one last time with the machete to end my life. I stayed in that position for almost 15 minutes. Then, I realized he – or someone else – had untied me. I was so shaken by that terrorizing incident that I made my mind up to leave the monster that day. This incident was only one part of a long-time pattern. Whenever he was drunk and wanted to show me that he was powerful, he would sit in front of me, grinding his teeth, and lay out all his knives and machetes and sharpen them. Then, he would run the blades across my body to test their sharpness. I had asked him many times to go for counseling, but he always refused. He would not talk to my pastor. He told me he had no problems. That night, I packed a few things, booked a flight, and left for Houston, Texas the next morning.

I came to Houston with a three-month-old baby boy, determined to return to New York later to get my daughter. I had left her with my aunt, who was living in my home with my husband. I knew my daughter would be safe with her. As crazy as my husband was, I knew he would never hurt my daughter. He loved her more than life itself. Still, I was worried about her.

I had visited Houston before, when the oil boom was in swing, and knew I could get a job there. I had borrowed some money from my aunt to start a new life Houston, but when I arrived, I had no job, no car, and no place to stay. My first day in Houston, as I sat crying in the lobby of the hotel where I was to stay the night, I met yet another Barbara, who saw me and came to me. I told her my story, and she offered me a place to stay. After a few days, I went for a job interview with her car. Twenty-two years later, Barbara and I are still friends.

The interview went well. I was told I was one of three hundred who had applied, and I would get a call back in a few days. While driving back from the interview, I saw an apartment, stopped, and filled out an application. I had so much faith that I would get the job that I wasn't worried how I would pay for it. The clerk told me I could have the apartment, but that the floor had just been shampooed, and was still wet. I said I would take it, but I wanted to move in right away. I walked to the mail box to put up a sign for a baby-sitter, and a girl picking up her mail said she would baby-sit for me. I told her I was moving in next door, but did not have a job yet and no money. She said, "It is okay. When you get paid, you will pay me."

This shows how I moved by faith. I did not have a job yet, but I knew God was giving that job to me. I got the apartment by faith, and when I went to the mailbox to post my sign, the baby-sitter was right there, offering to baby-sit. Then I wondered how I would get to work at my new job. I had no car, and in Houston, people must have transportation. I had only two hundred dollars left. My friend Barbara took me to her uncle and bought me a huge yellow Chrysler Cordoba for a fifty dollar down payment. I was so excited. I bought some garbage bags and spread them on the wet floors and laid myself and my three-month-old son Daniel down to sleep. We were the happiest people. I knew at the moment, everything was going to be all right, because God was in control. I was going to be safe from the torture king. I had left my life of negatives and danger.

The following Monday, I got the job as an accountant for eight companies. It was manual accounting, with no computers, and was very tedious. I did not get a salary for three weeks, since the first week was for training, with no pay. For the first three months, life was so difficult. I did not have enough money to feed my son properly, not even to buy him milk or diapers. I cut my skirts and used them for diapers, and gave him water and sugar instead of milk. I ate rice or crackers for weeks.

I had one plate, one cup, one spoon, one fork, and one small pot. Since I had no furniture, we sat – and slept – on the floor for months. Even through my poverty, I was so happy, full of peace and tranquility, and free of torture and abuse. Even though I had a house full of furniture in New York, I was more comfortable sleeping here, on the floor, on garbage bags. I know that you cannot put a price tag on peace, and I would not trade my peace for anything in this world.

Through many years of struggles and hard times, I knew that the Lord was always there with me, protecting me and guiding me. I always knew He was at my side. I felt His presence many times. I knew He carried me through the tough days when I felt there was no light at the end of the tunnel. My mother always told me to look for the silver lining beneath the dark clouds. Without faith, I would have been dead many years ago. Today, I feel blessed, with a lovely family. My daughter Michelle is thirty-one and has a lovely daughter, Alexia, age eleven. My son Daniel is twenty-two, and still lives with me. I was fortunate to be blessed with a chance to be trained for a job as a Revenue Agent with the IRS. My training and expertise enabled me to open my own practice, which I have run for the past twenty-one years. I consider myself successful in the tax field, where I assist taxpayers with IRS audits and IRS representation, tax preparation, real estate sales, tax consulting, managerial consulting, sales tax audits, and other tax problems. I am also blessed with the golden opportunity to witness and pray with many of my Christian clients and colleagues.

My current occupation allows me to continue to be a mediator in many areas. I am able to guide and assist individuals with their tax problems in the form of Offers and Compromises. Most people believe that there is no way to solve their problems, and because of this, their lives are miserable. I tell them that there are always solutions to problems, if they will just take their problems to the Lord in prayer. Many of my clients can attest to miracles worked within government circles. God works miracles through us and within us.

We are a blessing to ourselves and to others. Women who are living the kind of life I used to live should never feel that life is over. Life is just beginning. We just have to put an end to all the abuse and take control of our lives. If there are children involved, they are our responsibility. We cannot sit or lie there and let our lives die away to nothing, or our children will grow up without hope. But when we take God's hand and work to make our lives better – even when we don't feel much hope ourselves – we teach them how powerful faith is, and how it is possible to overcome anything.

We need to make each day count and live it to the fullest. I know that in an abusive relationship, whether mental or physical – and I have been "blessed" with both – we feel that life is gloomy. We feel depressed, and sometimes don't even recognize that we are depressed. When we lie and cry for hours and weeks and months, as I have done, that is depression. Try talking to God if you have no one else. He is your best friend. He is your only true friend. He does not judge you or criticize you or laugh at your mistakes. He will forgive you for your past and present. We may feel that we deserve our punishment, but now I can see this is not true. The devil makes us believe that. We can rise above the abuse. We can get our education. America is the land of opportunities, where education is available to us, if we are willing to work. With education, we can support ourselves and our children. We can leave the battered relationships and move on to a positive new future.

What are we teaching our children about respect? When they see us accepting the abuse, they think it is normal for them to accept it, too. We need to stop the abuse, not encourage it. Most women – and even some men – have experienced abuse. Yes, men too. In my practice, men have told stories to me of abuse, both mental and physical. So many of us keep it hidden due to fear of being ridiculed by others in our society. I lost my self-esteem for almost thirty-two years. I am now trying to rebuild it, but know that it can be very difficult to feel good and beautiful again when all you have known is ugliness.

Remember that with courage, a woman can fail at something, and go on to learn powerful lessons from her failures. We need to stand tall and be confident in ourselves and think positive. We can conquer anything we attempt – great or small – with God's guidance and acceptance, and in His time. God had a purpose for me. I still do not know what it is, but until I do, I will continue to be the best I can be in all things through Christ Jesus. Survival is ours. Claim it. Receive it, and let us rid the world of abuse by stopping the madness. We do not have to accept any more abuse, once we learn to believe in ourselves, to have more faith in ourselves, and to make a move. We cannot sit and wait for things to happen. We have to put things in motion, and trust that God will help direct our moves. Stop saying, "I wish I could do this," and get up and do it. So many of us believe we are failures. Even though we are not perfect, we are not failures unless we give up. We can correct our mistakes and move forward. Even though life is full of challenges, if you meet them head on, you can overcome them. I can tell you from my own experience that you will be glad you took that first step. It will be scary at first, but if I can do it, so can you. I am a foreigner, a female, a minority, and an abused woman. If I can be successful, so can you.

I have not yet reached my full potential, but I am striving to get there. My newest mentor is Lilliana Hickman Riggs. She is the accounting guru of Texas. She is the most positive role model for me. I admire and respect her very much. She makes me feel I can do anything and be anyone I want to be. Surround yourselves with positive role models, and stay away from people who are negative and depressing. Have faith mostly in yourself, and keep telling yourself, "I can do it." And never, ever forget the power of prayer. Overcoming my obstacles was only possible through faith and the power of prayer. My success gave me a burning desire to make a difference in this world for other women who have endured similar suffering and pain; to help them understand that they too can succeed in life through tough times and sacrifices. Never give up, have courage, and God will give you the grace to succeed in all things.

~ *Christina Dharamsingh*

Rod Shaw

Cindy Cline-Flores

Rod's Story

It was a scorching hot day in the summer of 1965, with temperatures exceeding the one-hundred-degree mark in the little town of Wharton, Texas. On this particular afternoon, a scrimmage game of football was being played, pitting the team from a four-year school against the players from Wharton Junior College, a two-year school. The four-year school had forty-eight players, while Wharton's team had less than twenty. The result was that, as the four-year school sent in fresh players every quarter, the Wharton team played the same few guys over and over. My brother, Rodney Shaw, the left halfback for Wharton, had been playing both quarterback and halfback for three hours that day, without a time-out or even a drink of water.

The whistle blew, and Rodney went out for a pass. He caught the ball but was immediately tackled hard by two large players, twisting his body in two directions as it was slammed to the ground. He immediately knew that something was dreadfully wrong. His first thought was, as he put it, that "they knocked my head off," because the only feeling he had was in his head and neck.

He lay on the ground in the heat for another two hours, waiting for an ambulance to come from a neighboring town with someone who knew how to move a person suspected of having suffered a spinal chord injury.

Rod was just nineteen years old, and was paying for his education by playing football on a sports scholarship. He had been All-State quarterback in high school and State AAA Collegiate quarterback, and had been voted most handsome by his freshman classmates. He had a beautiful girlfriend, and the world was his oyster – until that day.

Now he lay near death, ninety miles from the nearest trauma center and three hundred miles away from his family, his body going into shock and his mind completely alert to his condition, as the game continued to be played around him. When he finally reached the hospital, he was so near death that his family was told he would not live, and that even if he did, he would be a quadriplegic – paralyzed from the shoulders down – for the rest of his life.

It was a miracle that Rod did live, and he spent one year in a rehab hospital. His family was warned that he would likely withdraw from the world, never wanting to go out in public, and that he would be incapable of returning to college to finish his studies. In 1965 there were no provisions for one so impaired to function in the conventional world.

However, for the first of many times, Rod proved them wrong. One year later he enrolled in the University of Houston, and with the help of his mother, father, or sister, he was driven the thirty miles to his classes. There one of us would sit with him, taking notes and turning the pages of the books. Rod was a large person, 6 feet tall and 180 pounds. Our parents were small, just 5'2" and 5' 5," and in their late fifties. But they managed to lift him to dress him, and get him into and out of bed, cars, and wheelchairs. It was grief and struggle on a daily basis. But none of them ever gave up or gave in. Rod fought to live as normal a life as possible, and for two years he refused to believe that he would never have the use of his hands or feet again.

By 1968, however, he could see the physical toll this challenge was taking on his family, and he decided to write to all the major medical centers in the United States and inquire about what kind of independent living accommodations were available for the severely handicapped. Each and every one of them wrote back saying they knew of nothing. So he had two choices: live with his parents or go to a nursing home and live with the elderly.

For Rodney, neither of these was a satisfactory answer. He longed for independence. He wanted to drive, he wanted to date, he wanted to have his own privacy – and most of all, he did not want to be a burden to his family. But he was unable to walk or use his hands, and he needed help for all his personal hygiene, as well as for eating, taking meds, getting dressed and undressed, and moving about in the world.

Finally Rod decided to get together with three other boys he'd made friends with in rehab. They were all his age and all had been hurt playing sports. Together, the four of them created an alternative living plan that allowed the severely handicapped to live alone through the concept of shared attendant services. With Rod's leadership, these determined young men raised enough money from grants, and enough interest from the Texas Institute for Rehabilitation and Research, to open an eleven-bed model living facility that was fully adapted for handicapped living. The group incorporated as a 501.C3 nonprofit corporation, and called itself *Independent Lifestyles, Inc.*

Thus their idea became a reality. Nothing like it had ever been created. The first eleven people to live in this facility were all young men Rod's age, hurt in sports accidents in high school or college, who wanted to finish their education and live productive lives as normally as possible – the same thing that Rod and his partners wanted.

Cindy Cline-Flores

Two years later, in 1973, Rod and his friends had a commitment from a Houston builder to have 10% of the apartments in a new 350-unit apartment project built out for handicapped living – wide doors, roll-in showers, light switches and stove handles at waist high level. Door knobs were the French lever kind, and every room had an intercom that connected to an office housing a staff of caregivers on a 24-hour basis. It was the first of its kind in the nation.

One of these young men, George Broyles, had a brother who was a builder. In 1975 and 1976, Rodney spearheaded a campaign to raise over two million dollars to have George's brother build townhouses in the heart of Houston – the first ever to be owned by, and to have services for, the severely handicapped. In this environment, people could live nearly normal lives, get jobs, even have families. In fact, one young married woman who lived there became pregnant and had two children, which at that time was a first for a severely handicapped woman.

But I'm getting a bit ahead of myself. During this time Rodney wanted to learn to drive, but there was no device that would allow him to do so. There did exist a special gear box that enabled a paraplegic (someone who had use of his hands) to drive, but there was nothing for quadriplegics. But my brother was determined, so he enlisted the help of a friend, and together they modified the paraplegic gear box so that Rod could use it. Fortunately, a portion of Rod's arms did have some function, and he lifted sandbags attached to his biceps to strengthen them. Then he got a driving instructor to teach him how to drive. This whole operation took two years – but he did it, and in 1971 he bought a Pontiac, had it equipped and began to drive. Of course, someone had to lift him in and out of the car and strap his hands into leather gloves, which were then strapped onto the steering wheel. But he was as free as he could be, considering his severe impairment.

I must also tell you here that the junior college Rod had played for took no responsibility whatsoever for his injury nor his well-being, and there was no insurance, so our family bore the brunt of thousands of dollars worth of medical and rehabilitation bills and home renovation costs. So as my brother battled the daily routines of life that we take for granted, he struggled with his own finances too, while trying to keep Independent Lifestyles, Inc. alive and well through writing grants and asking for assistance from the state and federal governments.

The grants were written, and the next project was modifying housing to accommodate severely handicapped students on campus at the University of Houston. That dream became a reality, and modified housing with shared services was made available for twenty-five students to live on campus. By now there were five facilities around the city of Houston being managed by Rodney Shaw and Independent Lifestyles, Inc.

Meanwhile, Rod's desire to be independent behind the wheel of an automobile only grew, and before long he had another idea. Why not find people with the technical skills who could help him invent vans with electronic lifts so that people in wheelchairs could be easily lifted in and out of them? He also invented a van in which the floor could be lowered at the push of a button so that a person could stay in his or her wheelchair, roll under the steering wheel and drive without being transferred between the chair and the van's seat. Shortly after that, the Department of Human Services began using the vans with electronic lifts to offer transportation services for wheelchair-bound people who didn't own vehicles.

But now there was another problem: in those days, there was still no such thing as handicapped parking, and when Rod would park the van he couldn't get in and out of it because of cars parked next to his. The more mobile he became and the more places he wanted to go – sporting events, movies, etc. – the more he realized there were no accommodations for him once he arrived.

He began to work tirelessly to get handicapped parking legalized, along with curb cuts and ramps for wheelchair access. Even the design of the "handicap" logo you see on all of the parking spaces was taken from the logo that had been created for Independent Lifestyles, Inc.

By this time, Rod's three partners had earned their degrees in law and accounting and had gone on to other careers, so he was the only one left to continue the organization. But he never gave up. Often there was no money to pay himself, but he always believed things would work out and somehow, they always did.

My brother lived with his disability for twenty-two years, and in that time he changed the way the world related to the severely handicapped. He lobbied for the Americans With Disabilities Act, and for changes in the way the government supported our country's disabled veterans. The year he died, he went before the Texas Legislature to speak on behalf of the needs of senior citizens.

A year after Rod's death, at a celebration luncheon held in his honor, he was named Man of the Year by the Texas Rehabilitation Commission. A film was shown of his accomplishments, and only then did I realize all the organizations he had served and the causes he had championed. I was astonished! Even though I had worked closely with him on his advisory board and his as his financial officer, I still had not been aware of all he had accomplished. He had been tireless in his efforts to change the way the world perceived and supported the physically impaired.

Cindy Cline-Flores

My brother is my hero, and his story is an important illustration of living powerfully out of one's own passion and commitment. Rod was an ordinary man who accomplished extraordinary things because he refused to let anything keep him from experiencing everything life had to offer. He endured many hardships but he never gave up. He was a beacon of light and a tower of strength for all those who struggled for independence and the right to human dignity.

I feel my brother's life is a testament to the truth that when our goals, values and actions are in alignment, we also are in alignment with a power that is greater than our circumstances – and no illness, accident, or challenge of any kind has the power to defeat us. We were created to have dominion over our frailties, and we were given all the tools to be able to transcend any physical challenge.

The young men of this story who supported Independent Lifestyles and worked with Rodney were also remarkable human beings who accomplished incredible things in our world and in their own lives. They did so because theirs were spirits in rebellion against indifference, conventional medical wisdom, and well-meaning advice about living from the limitations of their physical impairments. They rebelled and dug down deep within themselves, calling forth a greater power than any of them knew, at least on an intellectual level, that they possessed. What was called forth in them is in every one of us as well. It is a greatness that we activate simply by being passionate about our purpose, and aligning all our actions with the intention of living that purpose.

I am thankful to my brother for showing me this truth. It is a lesson – a gift that will stay with me always.

~ Reverend Farolyn Mann

Photo by Alisa Murray

Gayle A Mueller
Photo by Alisa Murray

Cindy Cline-Flores

Going Forward
With Faith

I am a 64-year-old male, born in Cleveland, Ohio and raised Catholic. However, several years ago, I chose to practice a more spiritual path, rather than the ritual path that the Catholic Church offers. In 1975, I moved to Houston, Texas, where I remained until 1999. At that time, I returned to a suburb of my old hometown, and for the following three and a half years, I became the caretaker of my mother. It was during this time that I discovered water and aquatic programs at the local North Olmsted Community Center. I began using water exercise programs to help relieve some of the stress and anxiety that I was experiencing while taking care of my mother.

I am currently an Aquatics Specialist Instructor at the Memorial Hermann HBU/Wellness Center. As an employee at this wonderful center, I have created and developed programs that encourage members to live healthier lifestyles by reducing stress, eating nutritional foods, and maintaining proper weight balance.

I consider this to be my gift from God. My experiences as an Aquatics Specialist Instructor have helped me get through one of the most challenging experiences of my life. At the time I began taking water exercises in Ohio, I was over 250 pounds, and I am only 5' 7" tall. I was not a picture of good health.

The Beginning...

While I was a caretaker for my mother, I experienced several health challenges that soon became life-threatening. These episodes would begin with my throwing up blood, and finding blood in my stool. In addition, I would have flu-like symptoms, including high fevers and aches in my joints. When the first episode hit me in 1999, I thought at first it was caused by a bad corned beef sandwich. But that was not the case. After several days with a deteriorating condition, I went to the emergency room. A blood count revealed my hemoglobin count was 4, meaning 4 grams per deciliter. The normal hemoglobin count for an adult male is usually considered to be 14 to 16 grams per deciliter, so mine was seriously low. I spent a week in the hospital.

There were additional occurrences in 2000 and 2001. The doctors were able to stabilize me, but were never able to diagnose the exact problem; they finally concluded it was a form of varices. This is a bleeding condition resulting from chronic liver disease, usually caused by heavy drinking. The problem was that I did not fit that profile. My condition remained a mystery.

Locating the problem

In December of 2003, my mother fell, and I drove to Cleveland to be with her at the hospital. Her wish at that time was to die. But the injuries from her fall were corrected by surgery, and she was told that her chances of recovery were excellent. Her doctor stated that she was stable, and would be going back to the rehabilitation home. I stayed with my mother into January, when I had another occurrence and decided I needed to get back to Houston. I said my goodbye to my mom, promising to be back later in the year. A friend of mine in Houston strongly questioned me about my plans. He thought I was too ill to make such a long drive by myself. "You can't do this!" he protested. But I knew that I could make the trip, and I set out for Houston. My positive attitude and prayers were with me all the way, and I made it safely home.

Arriving in Houston, I called my doctor and saw him the next morning. He stated that I look like the walking wounded, and told me I was seconds away from dying. I spent another week in the hospital. Unfortunately, Mother made her transition the following week, in late January of 2004. I was sad, of course, but I was glad I'd had the chance to be with her towards the end of her life.

However, I knew it was now time to face my own health challenges. This time my doctor, Dr. Robert Davis, was determined to locate the cause of this problem. He began a series of periodic blood work, CAT scans, X-rays and a liver biopsy.

In late July, 2004, Dr. Davis informed me that he had brought in a specialist to work with us on my medical challenge. This was Dr. Rafael Botero, at the Texas Liver Center of the Memorial Hermann Medical Center. Two nodules had appeared on my liver, and they had doubled in size during the scheduled medical check tests that were run. Dr. Davis encouraged me to make an appointment at the Liver Center as soon as possible, so I scheduled an appointment for that month. I was encouraged to bring my nearest relative or closest friend with me to the appointment. I chose my closest friend, Joseph Smith, since my mother, my father, and my brother all had made their transitions.

Finally, a solution

Dr. Botero, the specialist, met with Joseph and me. Four other medical professionals were in the meeting as well. Dr. Botero explained to me that the nodules Dr. Davis referred to were cancerous. The internal bleeding problems that had occurred the previous four years were results of this cancer. It had been growing and spreading in the liver all of this time. While the news was certainly not good, I was actually relieved to finally know what the real problem was, and that there was a potential solution. Joseph, however, was in shock, not only from the news of the liver cancer, but from my reaction of relief. Dr. Botero informed me that a Dr. Hadar Merhav would be coming in to talk to us more about the solutions.

Dr. Merhav told us that I would first have to go through a surgical procedure, RFA (radio frequency ablation). Then, if that was not successful, I would need a liver transplant. Two weeks later, I had the RFA. This procedure reduced the size of the cancer, but they had found that there was more than one type of cancer, and there was more of it than had showed up in the previous X-rays and MRIs. Dr. Merhav was not sure about one of the cancers, which he called very aggressive. He said that there was a 98% chance of that cancer returning.

The transplant

Within a few weeks, the cancer did return. By this time I began having problems with anemia. Surprisingly, though, I looked very healthy and showed no outward signs of having liver problems. I was put on the transplant list, and received a letter to inform me of that.

Joseph, who has Chaplaincy training, agreed to be my primary caretaker through the process. We began to meet other medical professionals, who eventually became our "Transplant Team." They were all wonderful, and guided us through the process of being a candidate for a liver transplant. To go into detail about the process would take another whole book; all I can tell you is that it is an overwhelming experience from every standpoint – medically, logistically and financially, as well as psychologically, emotionally and spiritually.

We had been meeting with our transplant team for only two weeks – educating ourselves on transplants and gathering a support team to assist with my recovery process after the transplant – when we received news that there was a liver available. It just so happened that Joseph and I were together that day and we were both able to report to the hospital at the same time. Unfortunately, after about four hours, we were informed that the liver was not a good match, after all.

But I continued to hold out hope. After another three weeks, I got a call at the Wellness Center. There was another liver, this one more promising. I called Joseph, who was having his car serviced at the time. I reported to the hospital first, and Joseph arrived a few minutes later.

This time, it turned out to be a "go," and I had the transplant on October 14, 2004.

The recovery

My recovery from the transplant went better than anyone anticipated. I was in ICU a day and half, and on the transplant recovery floor three days. My total time in the hospital was six days. Two weeks after the transplant, my recovery increased rapidly. Medicines were reduced or eliminated, and I was given permission to resume my normal lifestyle. In my fifth week, I made plans to return to work. I began to drive my car again, and returned to work in my sixth week.

The numerous individuals that had volunteered to assist with my recovery were not needed. Joseph was able to handle all of the challenges that came up. He took great care of me when needed.

The surgery scar healed very quickly, and I anticipated that it would be hardly anything to look at in a year's time.

Faith

I have always had a positive attitude. This comes from faith in myself and in a Creator who assists me in co-creating a wonderful life for myself. This Creator, whom I call Father, is always there to help me think and work through any challenge that I have encountered in life. Receiving the news of the liver and the transplant could have been devastating to me. However, I knew that if I were to make it through this problem successfully, I just had to move out of the way, and let the Father take charge.

Joseph initiated a huge prayer support group to pray for a positive and successful outcome to the transplant. Later I learned that thousands of individuals from all walks of faith joined in this prayer support. Several prayer teams were formed through the Wellness Center by email and word of mouth – all praying for the same outcome. Members and individuals also donated blood in my name. There was even a group who were on a cruise who had learned of my situation and took time to join in prayer for my recovery.

Knowing that these prayers were being said helped me continue with my positive attitude and recovery. These prayers from individuals I didn't even know encouraged me to pursue a rapid recovery. I found that all obstacles came down, positive thinking rose, and I was filled with gratitude. These factors healed me in ways and in places that even medicine couldn't touch.

Now in my prayers I thank everyone for being there for me. Also, I pray for the individual whose liver I received, as well as that person's family. For I will never know who they were. But I owe my life to them.

I affirmed what I have been practicing as a wellness instructor, that a healthy body and mind were not created to be waited on or babied. You must go forward with determination and faith that the Father will make sure that all goes well. And it surely doesn't hurt to have good doctors, good friends, and a few hundred prayers and good wishes as well.

~ *Gayle A Mueller*

Sharron Border and Katie
Photo by Short Street Photographers

Cindy Cline-Flores

Katie Svetla's Story

I knew.... I knew right away. They say that it never happens like that. They say it takes time to know that this child is "your child." But I knew right away that Svetla was my daughter. That's why I gave her the little yellow dress. It came from my sister Marsha, with instructions to give it to my daughter when I found her. I found Svetla in an orphanage in Bulgaria in September 1991. She was three years old and living in her third orphanage.

The 1990s were an unstable time in Bulgaria and in all of Eastern Europe. Communism was failing and poverty was commonplace. The winters were harsh, and I was told that there was little food and heat in the government controlled orphanages. Staffing in the orphanages was in short supply, so there could be only minimal interaction with the children.

The day that I found Svetla, I had traveled to the orphanage with a translator. When the staff brought Svetla out to meet

me, she was very shy and somewhat wary, but her big brown eyes met mine. I gave her a doll that she loved immediately. I sat on the floor with Svetla in my lap, and she seemed so pleased to be hugged. I didn't know at the time that I was the first visitor she'd ever had. I visited for 30 minutes when the translator told me that it was time to leave. I was sad to leave Svetla, but I hugged her goodbye and left the day room. A few minutes later, it occurred to me that someone should take a photograph of Svetla and me, because I was beginning to feel that I wanted to adopt her, and the Bulgarian government needed proof that we had actually met. I went outside and found her on the porch eating a slice of bread and cheese. When Svetla spotted me, she jumped up and down in excitement, threw the bread and cheese aside, ran toward me, and threw her arms around me. That's when I knew that Svetla was going to be my daughter.

We had two brief visits before I returned to the United Sates to finalize the adoption. The last visit was the hardest, because someone had prematurely told Svetla that I was her "Mama," and that I was going to take her home with me. My heart was breaking when I left the orphanage that last time, because Svetla was holding her arms out to me, screaming, "Mama, Mama," while the staff held her tightly and led her away.

After a long process, including the government changing from communism to democracy, the Bulgarian government approved Svetla's adoption. She was so excited to see me in January 1992, when I arrived to take her to the United States. After we finished all our paperwork, the American Consulate told me that Svetla was the first healthy Bulgarian child to be adopted by an American.

Svetla adapted quickly to her new life in America. In fact, she soon understood that Svetla was not your typical American name, and when I suggested a number of other first names, she seemed to delight in calling herself Katie. So Katie Svetla became her American name.

Soon Katie Svetla started preschool. She was learning, but it became apparent that she didn't have the skills and abilities shown by even younger children. True, she didn't speak English, but soon we discovered that Katie didn't have any language skills, including the ability to speak Bulgarian. It's understandable. During those early years, when parents were continually talking and reading to their children, adults were only infrequently talking to Katie. So how could she possibly have learned Bulgarian? In the orphanage, she had no toys. So, while the children in her preschool were coloring "masterpieces" for their parents, Katie didn't even know how to hold a crayon.

Kindergarten was a struggle for Katie. She cried every morning and begged me not to send her to school, because she felt "dumb." In first grade, she was referred to the school psychologist for a battery of achievement tests. The results were devastating. The school psychologist told me that Katie would not be able to complete a regular high school curriculum. She also said that Katie would not "catch up," and that the effects of deprivation in her early life made her future look bleak. I was in a state of shock for weeks afterwards.

After the shock wore off, I decided that we needed to challenge these assumptions about a little girl who deserved so much more. Katie and I launched into a myriad of activities that included speech therapy, innovative reading and math programs, and special education services. These programs were met with both enthusiasm and frustration by Katie. She lit up when she was successful; at other times, she struggled, cried and emotionally beat herself up. Some days – in fact, many days – both of us felt like giving up. Yet Katie persevered.

Cindy Cline-Flores

Then in sixth grade, it seemed like the light dawned. The years of hard work were paying off. She began to earn A's and B's; and most remarkably she made the Honor Roll. Katie could not have been prouder (nor could I). She continued to receive extra help in school, but services were gradually decreased, then ultimately taken away. She was making it on her own! And through it all, a hidden talent had emerged. The little girl who didn't know how to hold a crayon had become a talented artist.

When Katie was a junior in high school, she received the greatest gift of her life up until then – an honor so amazing that she never dared to dream it was possible. That was the day that Katie walked across the candlelit stage of her high school auditorium and was inducted into the National Honor Society, an honor based on scholarship, character, leadership, and service. No one could have been prouder or more deserving than Katie. And her mom – well, through her tears, she couldn't stop beaming from ear to ear.

~ *Sharron Border*

Marion Wilkholm

Cindy Cline-Flores

The Sit-Up Comedienne

In the summer of 1954, hope was everywhere. It didn't occur to me that it could or would ever be any other way. Then, in August, three months after my eighth birthday, I contracted lumbar polio, which left me paralyzed from the waist down. As it turns out, losing the use of my legs was small compared to the fact that I lost all hope. I lost my hope of ever running, jumping, skating, or being the jump rope champion of my class again. I lost my hope of being able to be "normal" like most everyone else. Most of all, I lost the hope of having a good and productive life, as I had lost the hope of believing in myself anymore. My physical prowess had always been my salvation, and that was no more.

The last picture of me standing

Nearly sixty years have now passed, and I can honestly say that I have fully recovered. Oh, I still walk with crutches, and often use my wheelchair – especially when I do my "Sit-Up Comedy" presentations! The best realization of all is that I have fully recovered my hope. Hindsight has shown me that after contracting polio, my mind had been much more paralyzed than my legs. True paralysis is being without hope. It is the most painful loss of all. Hope is what I stand for today (or as I say in my comedy show, what I sit for). My comedy presentations are a symbol of the hopefulness I now have towards life. I have even gone so far as to creating a comedy CD entitled *Taking a Bite Out of Adversity – with Humor.* I have learned over the years that adversity is quite an influential teacher, especially when it comes to hope, or lack of it.

Come with me to my little hometown in Bird Island, Minnesota. It was the summer of my eighth year, and it was (to borrow an old phrase) truly the best of times, and the worst of times. It was the summer in which I learned how to ride my two-wheeled bicycle, how to roller skate, and most of all, I learned that if anything got too stressful, I could run it off, or skip away – even from adversity. It was also the summer of the polio epidemic. Over one week's time that August, everything changed. Steps that I had taken four at a time, I could no longer take, even one at a time. I particularly remember the morning when I awakened without a leg to stand on. That was the beginning of many dark days that turned into dark weeks, and eventually, months and years. I remember being miserable, depressed, and bitter most of the time. Most of all, I remembered being without hope. I lived that way – if you want to call that living – for ten years, until I was eighteen years of age.

After graduating from Tulane University School of Social Work, I became a practicing social worker, in the psychiatric arena. I have been a social worker for over forty years, and love my work and the people I work with. It has been a wonderful and gratifying experience. Then, some years ago, I had the opportunity to take a "Stand-Up Comedy" course at the University of New Orleans. (I'll tell you a little more about that in a while.) Now, when something adverse happens to me, I ponder it, work on resolving the issue, and do some (reasonably) respectful comedy about it. Not only do I feel better, but my audience seems to enjoy reliving the experience with me, all with a comical but truthful twist. Comedy is a way to maintain a more objective perspective about problems, while making those problems seem less daunting at the same time.

I am a believer. I now believe in practical, everyday ways to reassemble the hope that one loses when adversity hits them head-on – or even if it sneaks up and attacks them from behind! The very first step is to become ready to deal with your situation, whatever that may be. As a psychotherapist, I know that you have to be ready to face your problem. It is important to assess where you are, and get help, which is often necessary, in making yourself ready to deal with the adversity. Many well-intentioned people insist that they know when the time is right for you, saying that you need to take action immediately. What they are overlooking is that each of us must handle our problems in our own way, and according to our own schedule. In my life, from the time I was eight years old until I was eighteen, I was stuck in my hopelessness, and firmly believed that there was no way out, primarily because I could never walk normally again.

But I'm getting ahead of myself. Let me backtrack a little. That I even entered college was obviously by the grace of God, as I had not applied myself throughout my high school career, but did just enough to get by. Even though I had literally worked very hard at denying myself the opportunity to attend college, I was accepted at St. Catherine's College in St. Paul, Minnesota. The fact that I had gotten into the school planted a new seed of hopefulness in me that had been absent throughout my young life. I was extremely excited with my new environment, and with having a fresh opportunity to change the way I saw my life and the world around me. To be sure, there were plenty of new challenges to face. I had to get up steps the best way I could, and get from building to building in a wheelchair, which I had never considered using before. I began my school year on scholastic probation, because my grades in high school had not been that good. Well, they weren't that great in college either, at least not at first. Truth be told, I was having such a grand time that I forgot to study! I received a reality lesson when my advisor came to me in the fall of my sophomore year, and told me that if I did not significantly improve my grades, I would have to leave St. Catherine's by the end of the semester.

My spirit was crushed, and all my new-found hope seemed to go out the window once more. That was the year that President Kennedy was assassinated, and I remember feeling like I, too, was riddled with bullets, though of a different kind. I identified with the President for many reasons, primarily because he was himself disabled by serious back trouble. Yet there emerged in me a small spark of hope that I could make something good of his untimely death. And from that small spark, I found determination once again to make every effort to improve my life. I studied night and day after that, and was able to get my grades up to a good level. Truly, the inspiration was phenomenal, and that spirit of hope and determination stayed with me throughout my college experience. In many other ways too, my college experience helped me see that I had choices and decisions to make that would greatly affect my life. I even learned to look at my physical disability in a different light. Instead of concentrating on what I could not do, I learned to focus on what I could do, and build on that. It even occurred to me that having a disability could help me be more empathetic towards others who had a disability, even if their disability was not physical. In addition, I learned to hope that I could become a good role model for other people, and a source of hope for them, much like President Kennedy had been for me.

In the process of attempting to help other people, I inadvertently strengthened my own "hope muscles" again. I also learned to use my mind to overcome the mental paralysis I had sustained for so long. It was amazing to me to realize that prior to college, I had considered myself a total victim, feeling that there was nothing I could do to better myself. Sometimes, it feels so good to be wrong, and this was one of those times! My "Awakening 101" course, and those that followed, taught me that my real problem was not so much the disability as the way that I had perceived it. I had painted the name of JFK's boat – *PT 109* – across the back of my wheelchair, and in my yearbook under the picture, the publishing staff wrote, "Sometimes you have to lose your life in order to find it." Sometimes you have to lose your hope before you can appreciate what a great asset it is, and how important it is to find ways to expand that wonderful virtue to encompass your whole life.

Improving my grades gradually opened the door to graduate school. After my graduation from college, I moved to New Orleans, Louisiana to attend Tulane University. I still did not have a lot of confidence in myself, because my self-esteem still needed bolstering, but I loved graduate school as much as I had loved my undergraduate years. As I mentioned earlier, I learned to be a social worker there, a career I have worked in and loved for more than four decades. I even say in my comedy presentations that people actually pay me to convince themselves that their problems are worse than mine. It was in graduate school that I learned to actually laugh at the irony of my own – and others' – disabilities, and to teach others to take their own problems less seriously. What a glorious experience that was. For the first time, my hope of being of service to others was being fulfilled. I was learning how to reach out to others therapeutically. It also helped me see the need to deal positively with my own problems, and to prepare myself for a whole new future. I became involved in individual therapy, which encouraged me to begin taking action, instead of just hoping for the best. Determination, appropriate action, persistence, and hope are an excellent combination of traits, each of which needed to be rekindled and nourished in my life. I have always loved my work, providing guidance to individuals within their family and environmental system. I have worked with all age groups, and enjoyed learning and growing right along with my clients – growing in faith, in compassion and understanding, and always, in hope.

As for my personal life, my hope was always to have a family of my own. I married Ronald in December of 1974, and we have two children. There were certainly many challenges in our marriage, starting with the fact that my husband had eyesight problems, and could not drive a car for the first fifteen years of our marriage. Then, in 1989, he had a lens implant, which improved his vision sufficiently to allow him to begin driving. My own disability slowed me down physically and, at the same time, taught me to be resourceful. In order to get pregnant with my first child, I had to go to the finest fertility specialist in New Orleans, Dr. Richard Dickey. After giving birth, I developed a blood clot in my bad leg. My husband responded to this by putting ribbons and a big red sign out on the lawn that said, "It's a clot!" And here I thought that I was the comedian in the family! When the children were little, I would put them on a leash and let the dog run free, because the dog minded better! The children and I had our disabled moments too, but we worked

A "Sit-Up Comedienne" at work!

Cindy Cline-Flores

together to overcome problems. They are both grown now, and doing well. Hope definitely helped me have and enjoy my family.

In 1995, I reached another turning point. I participated in a "Stand Up Comedy" course offered at the University of New Orleans, taught by Mike Parnon, a professor of architecture, where I earned sixteen Rubber Chicken units! Mike very skillfully worked with people in the class, helping them learn to tell their personal stories in a humorous manner. I took the six-week non-credit course, then hired Mike to help me as my personal humor coach. We got together every week and worked on making things that had happened to me or my family into something comical for everyone to enjoy.

Adversity is like the thick gray clouds that fill the sky and contribute to our feelings of hopelessness. Finding the humor in adversity is that spark of hope that helps us soar through the clouds and find the sun shining on the other side. Instead of experiencing my disability as a curse that seems to cripple me, as I did early in my life, I now see that it is a tool that I can use to find hope in everyday situations. That which I used to cry about now represents another invitation to have hope. There is hope that there are lessons to be learned in life, and there is always a bit of humor to be realized as soon as you are able to get through the clouds and find the sun again.

Faith in God and hope have not always been my sidekicks, but they are ever-present now. Prayer and meditation are essential ingredients in keeping faith and hope alive within my heart and my spirit. I used to be mad at God for allowing me to have polio, but now I realize that polio has been a gift. It is my lifelong guide to helping others find hope in their lives, and a constant reminder of what I need to be, do, and have (in that order) in my life to keep my own hope alive and vibrant.

~ *Marion Wilkholm*

Chhay Mak with his beloved grandmother
Photo by Alisa Murray

Cindy Cline-Flores

The Flame At Arm's Length: A Journey To Freedom

I was born on July 3, 1973 in a small, tropical Southeast Asian country called Cambodia. In 1975, the totalitarian Communist Khmer Rouge assumed control of my country and ruled for four long years. During its bloody reign, nearly one in four Cambodians was executed or died from forced labor, starvation, or disease. The regime's disastrous attempts at agricultural reform led to mass starvation, and its insistence on total self-sufficiency for Cambodia deprived the people of necessities such as medical supplies and treatment. Hence, many died of preventable or treatable diseases. All told, the Khmer Rouge was one of the most lethal regimes of the twentieth century.

There remain many blanks in my story, but I guess it really began when I was about two years old and struck with the polio virus. Most people in developed countries have forgotten what a nightmare polio can be, since it was all but eradicated in their world. In Cambodia, we weren't so lucky. I am told that I was running and playing outside one day, and someone noticed that I started to drag my left foot. Then, a bit later, I fell to the ground, and within a few hours, I had a very high fever. Over a short period of time, I lost movement in all my limbs, and my ability to move my head was impaired as well. I could only move my facial muscles. Slowly I began to regain movement, but I could no longer walk, much less run.

At the time the Khmer Rouge came to power, I had only recently recovered from the initial effects of the polio. By rights, I should have been killed because I couldn't walk, and was therefore of no use to the Party. In fact, members of my community are amazed that I'm alive today. Everyone says that I should have been shot dead, as were so many other handicapped and impaired citizens. At any rate, I was spared. And I have to say that being handicapped during the Killing Fields period had its advantages – for me, at least – as well as its disadvantages. Since I couldn't walk, I didn't have to labor in the fields, and was left alone all the time to stare out the window and think. I was lonely, but my loneliness afforded me the opportunity to think about and decide who I would be inside, and laid a foundation for a lifelong tendency toward introspection, setting the stage for my own form of spirituality. I taught myself patience early on, because no matter what, I couldn't change one single thing that went on during the day. I figured out that the only things I could choose at any moment were my inner thoughts and focus. My thoughts were totally up to me, so I learned to shut out the world, fantasizing about whatever I wanted. For me, therefore, the chaos of the Khmer Rouge regime and the sounds of war were little more than background noises.

Though too young to realize it at the time, I was not only meditating, but was also practicing some of the principles of Buddhism. What was instilled in me was that life is just inner emotions, and the outside world doesn't matter, no matter how evil or how good it is perceived to be. It's all in your mind. So for me, hope became a very real thing. Having no control over the outside world, I had very little except hope, and perhaps as a consequence, I've always hoped and believed that things would turn out just fine.

I was not totally alone all of the time, of course. My saving grace in so many ways was my grandmother. Like most of the others, she worked in the fields all day, and the workers were fed a subsistence diet of watery rice soup. The soup was so thin you could count the grains of rice in your bowl. Although I couldn't work and therefore wasn't entitled even to those meager rations, my grandmother always made sure I got a bowl of that rice soup. When she couldn't bring it to me herself, she would make sure to send it with my brother or one of my cousins. I always got a full portion – not a bit less. It overwhelms me to think about this because I now realize that in those days, my grandma was sure I wouldn't survive, yet she still made sure I got my soup every day and that I wasn't cheated out of any of it. Frankly, given the circumstances, I would have understood if she had kept a little extra for herself or had given it to someone else, but she never did. Whenever she was able to find and sneak any extra food, she always shared that with me too. To this day that astounds me. My grandmother played such a vital role in keeping me alive.

I also remember a cat she had. She and that cat enjoyed a special bond. Sometimes at night the cat would hunt for mice in the sugar cane fields surrounding our hut, and when it would capture one, it would bite off its head. Instead of eating the mouse, the cat would often carry its tiny body into the hut and lay it gently next to my grandma as she slept. I'm sure that other people who have outdoor cats have experienced something like this, and I imagine most people are a little grossed out by it, even though the cat is doing it with the best of intentions. But remember, we were desperate for anything that was even marginally edible, so this little offering was quite welcome. My grandma would often find a way to secretly cook the mouse and share it with us. It was a gift of love from her cat, a gift that she passed on to us. I still find it amazing that even in the darkest of days, love still finds a way to shine its light.

In December 1978, Vietnam invaded Cambodia, and the Khmer Rouge was forced to retreat to the countryside. My family, along with hundreds of other families, began the journey towards a refugee camp in Thailand. At first, I was left in Cambodia with some relatives I didn't know, the plan being to leave me there while my folks decided whether or not things would indeed be all right at this new place. If they decided to stay, they would send for me. I remember thinking that the people I lived with were not my family, but I just couldn't bring myself to ask who they were. After all, in my world, silent acceptance was a child's duty.

About a month after my family left for the camp, they sent for me. Before dawn one morning, a man came to pick me up on a bike that had a metal rack on back. It was a very long ride, but I remember being very happy and excited, although I did not allow myself to let my excitement show. We were riding through some rough terrain, and I was afraid that my feet would go into the spokes, since I had no control over them. My legs swung helplessly as we rode, and although I was scared, I didn't say anything. I just hung on and hoped for the best. Finally, the man noticed my predicament, and asked me why I hadn't said anything. With some effort, I answered him, though I could not bring myself to look him in the eyes. I wanted to avoid being any trouble at all, and didn't want to give him any reason not to take me to my mom. After pondering a bit, he came up with a solution to my problem. He tied a small tree branch to the bike, then tied my feet to the branch. The problem was that he had the tops of my feet against the branch, rather than having the soles resting on top of it. Once my feet were secured and we had set off again on our journey, I learned the meaning of real pain. As the bike wheels bounced over the jagged terrain, the tops of my feet were constantly scraped against the rough surface of the bark, and before long, the skin was rubbed completely raw. Though it was agonizing, I didn't say a word, and I suppose that for a long time the man just assumed everything was fine.

Finally, without turning around, he asked me if I was okay, and I respectfully replied, "Yes." I basically decided to consciously hallucinate, focusing my mind elsewhere, virtually removing myself from the bicycle, the bumpy road, and the awful pain. And it worked; somehow I got through that long bike trip without betraying my suffering. I was ecstatic when I finally reached my family. At that moment, I truly forgot about the pain – that is, until they poured some sort of medicine or alcohol on my wounds. Let me tell you: it burned, and badly. But man, was I happy.

I remember this incident so vividly because I was and still am very proud of myself for having been able to handle the situation at that young age. In fact I often point back to this moment as being instrumental in my ability to handle the excruciating pain and suffering that I would have to endure later in my adult life. Human beings are amazing, and the mind is an astonishing thing. Even in the midst of physical or mental pain you can start by focusing on something else to begin easing it. Then have faith and know – decide – that it will be okay. After all, you have overcome situations before. There is no reason for you not to believe or have faith that you can do it again. The essence of the human spirit is that we overcome. Sometimes, we all momentarily forget, but we must never allow ourselves to forget completely.

Coming to America

My family lived in the refugee camp for three long years. I have many memories of that time, including my first real memories of my father. My dad was a gregarious guy, a real charmer whom everyone in the camp liked, but he was also a ladies' man whose numerous indiscretions sometimes got him in trouble and hurt my mom terribly. My father and I spent a lot of time together, though; he took me around the camp and got the people there to accept me. He really brought out my personality.

One of my clearest memories of camp life was the constant awareness of being fenced in, separated from the rest of the world. I would look at the highway on the other side of the fence and wonder where it led. I would sometimes see white people passing by – doctors, mostly – and think they were angels. In a very real sense, they were. I would watch vehicles zooming by, and they seemed magical. Where were they going? What was the world like outside of that fence?

I was soon to find out.

As you might imagine, the goal of the refugees was to get out of the crowded and often dangerous camps to some place where they could live a safe and normal life. Unfortunately, a safe and normal life did not seem possible in Cambodia, so most people set their sights for other countries, including the US, Australia, France, Canada, and several other countries. People registered for refugee status, and then could do little but wait to see if their names would be called to go. Relocation required sponsorship by someone in the new country – an individual, a group, or an institution such as a church. Unfortunately, most families got separated during this process, though it was highly unusual for a parent to be separated from a child. However, it was also a sad fact that most people didn't get "sponsored out," and many had to return to Cambodia.

In 1981, my uncle's family got sponsored to go to America, and my mother had to make the decision to let my brother leave with them. My mom felt she that she had to give at least one of her children a chance at a better life. I am sure it was one of the most painful choices she ever had to make. But in 1983 the remaining members of my family finally got called. It was both a joyful and frightening time for us. To begin with, there was the fifteen-hour plane ride; my mom was so scared she held on to me the whole time. I remember our descent into San Francisco so clearly: I looked out the window into the night, and thought it was some sort of heaven. Lights were everywhere. You can imagine the contrast to what I had been seeing… oh, my gosh. I was in total awe. I didn't know what to make of it. I was nearly in shock, although I was careful to conceal it.

At this point, I couldn't speak any English. I attended an all-handicapped school, where I got to pick out a wheelchair. It was the coolest thing. I also managed to work out a deal where I would assist with washing dishes in the school cafeteria after lunch was over. I would get ice cream as my payment, while the other kids went back to class. I also learned how to cook for the first time, and fell in love with it. I loved being able to do a lot of things that interested me. I was so happy to be alive, and learning new things added to my joy.

Meanwhile, my dad continued to be "the man." My mom finally got tired of all the lies and the disrespect, and in 1985 we left him. We just pulled up roots and moved to Houston, which has a sizeable Asian population but only a small Khmer community. Although I really only knew my father for about six years, I realize that he has had a lasting influence on me, in both good ways and bad.

No "happily ever after"

Coming to America wasn't the end of my story; it was just the beginning. Houston was much better than Cambodia, of course, but life remained challenging for us. We continued to be strangers in a strange land, and were still poor, sharing a home with two other families. I attended programs at various churches so I could have somewhere safe to explore new things and make new friends. I was always running around a lot, and being "confined" to a wheelchair didn't faze me. After my early years spent barely surviving in the jungle, I didn't look upon much of anything as an obstacle.

My English was coming along, but in 1986, when I was in middle school, I was still spending most of my time with other handicapped kids. The rest of the student population was normal, but all the kids in my homeroom were disabled. That was just the way it was. We all went to lunch together and got stared at all the time, and although I always remained outwardly composed, the silent stares bothered me. Moreover, my English was still not that great, which further set me apart from the rest of the student population. I was, however, excelling in my studies, and towards the end of the school year, I was attending a couple of regular classes.

The turning point for me came when I was introduced to an adaptive sports organization, a group devoted to promoting sports for people with disabilities. It was called the Houston Challengers, not to be confused with the girls' basketball team of the same name. I was impressed that something like that even existed, and it was ultimately through my involvement in this organization a few years later that I would come to realize that I had athletic capabilities. I moved to another school in 1987, when I was fourteen, but this time I attended regular – albeit English as a Second Language (ESL) – classes. At least I didn't have to be stuck in all-handicapped classes for the entire day, although my homeroom was still made up of only handicapped students. By the end of the year, I was attending regular English classes, and I actually received a school award.

Though we were making a lot of progress by this time, my family was still poor, living in government housing, and my wardrobe was still pretty limited. I wore sweats or secondhand blue jeans to school. I did have a sleeveless aqua Ocean Pacific shirt that I particularly liked (remember, this was the 1980s!), and I wore it often. In fact, that's what I wore to the award ceremony at the school. But as soon as we got there, I felt the heat from people staring at us. I know they were wondering why I was dressed like that when everyone else was dressed up. Suddenly I was embarrassed. My mom and I sat in the back of the room, and when my name was called, I just pretended I didn't hear it.

By 1988, I was in high school, and attending all regular classes. To my joy, the school offered an adaptive physical education class, which I took, of course. I loved sports, and was soon outperforming everyone in the class. Towards the end of 1989, the coach told me about an organization that offered wheelchair sports. It turned out that this was the organization I had first learned about a couple of years earlier, the Houston Challengers. I signed up with Metro Lift, the Houston public transportation system's special service for disabled riders, so I could get to the games and play. Not only did this give me an opportunity to play the sports I loved; it allowed me to get away from the crazy neighborhood I lived in. I signed up for every sport I could, and before long I was winning track and field meets left and right. I played basketball and wheelchair team handball (which eventually morphed into today's popular indoor wheelchair soccer). I started winning at regional and even national meets, using racing chairs that were twice my body size.

In 1990 I was awarded a custom track chair for being an outstanding athlete in the Southwest Region. The man who made the decision to award me that prize was the late Jim Hayes, a true pioneer in the disability community, who passed away in May of 2008. Coach Hayes was in a wheelchair himself for most of his life, the result of a spinal cord injury when he was only eighteen, and he spent his career mentoring students with physical and mental disabilities. At the time he made the decision that would help change my life, he was the president of the Southwest Athletic Association (SWAA). When I got the custom track chair, I was setting national records as a junior athlete. I was also good enough to compete against the adults at their nationals. At the same time, I was excelling in junior wheelchair basketball in Pasadena, Texas. I was involved with sports five days a week. I later began participating in and winning road races. I even won some money, and got recognition from the local NBC affiliate station.

Life was getting better all the time.

A party animal

In 1991, thanks in large part to a good friend of mine who took me to visit the campus, I received a scholarship to the University of Texas at Arlington (UTA), where the aforementioned Jim Hayes was a coach. UTA offered full athletic scholarships for intercollegiate wheelchair basketball, and I was fortunate enough to get one.

On my very first night at UTA, I attended a huge party. This was something completely new to me. In contrast to the outgoing fellow I had been under my father's tutelage in the refugee camp in Thailand, I had become very shy and timid in America. Up till now, I had put most of my passion and energy into playing sports. Partying was something I didn't know how to do. Well, I got broken in very quickly, and partying soon became second nature. Although I didn't have much experience with women either, that soon changed as well. Before long, basketball, parties, and women had become my life.

As for school, however, I became complacent. I slacked off quite a bit on my studies, often putting my academic status, and therefore my eligibility for the sport I loved, in jeopardy. Time and time again, I found myself scrambling to keep my grade point average high enough so I would be eligible to play the following semester. To tell the truth, I found school boring, except for the sports part, of course, and I missed many classes. I was too consumed by other things to let myself be bothered with studying. Much of the time I was preoccupied with proving all of the naysayers wrong – the people who told me, over and over, that I couldn't do this or that because I was in a wheelchair. As I became increasingly obsessed with proving them wrong, I became my dad and ten times worse. Yet no one – not even my coach – ever took me aside for a serious talk. I suppose everyone always assumed I would be okay, despite the tightrope I was walking. I guess they were right, because I always managed to pull it off somehow. I was never scared, and I always believed in myself. Many times I put myself in a precarious situation just to see if I could pull it off. In retrospect I can see how foolish I was, but the truth is that even today, I sometimes still struggle with this tendency. Maybe I just want to make sure I remain ready for anything, and that I'm always able to improvise in case I need to do so. In a way, these challenges I set for myself help boost my self-confidence, or at the very least, help me to ignore any self-doubt.

As for the basketball team, UTA won four straight National Championships, in three of which I played a part. We were so dominant that we ranked as high as fifth among the National Wheelchair Basketball Association (NWBA). We were constantly in the media; we were the big men on campus, and everything came easily to us. Fans were always at the airport to send us off when we went on trips or to receive us when we returned, and we were on national TV shows such as *The Today Show*, and a PBS documentary. We were even honored by President Bill Clinton. We were definitely living the life. I was not only experiencing things people had said I shouldn't even think about, but I was going way, way beyond that.

I guess you could say it all caught up with me in my fourth and final year at UTA. This had been our team's most dominant year and continuing victory seemed a sure thing. Well, life is funny; it has a way of teaching you lessons, especially when you become complacent. My lesson came in the form of the very last game I played against The University of Illinois for the championship. I was really looking forward to that game, and to getting my fourth championship ring. Once that happened, I could rightfully claim I was undefeated throughout my college career. I was playing my best game, my shots falling like rain. We were full of confidence, having beaten The University of Illinois earlier in the year by more than 30 points. PBS had been following the season for their documentary, which they called "Drive for Five." I personally was so confident I even had my roommate write "5-Peat" on my shoulder, which PBS captured.

Although I was playing my best game ever, we were off as a team, and were behind for 95% of the game. With only nine seconds left, we finally tied the other team. Even at that late hour, I absolutely believed that we would win it in overtime, because we were finally playing real UTA ball. Then, the other team inbound the ball, and the time ticked to zero seconds when the center threw up a hook shot with his back towards the basket… and the ball went in as the buzzer sounded. To quote an often-repeated phrase, we managed to snatch defeat from the jaws of victory. And that was the beginning of another difficult period in my life.

When the party's over...

After that disappointing season, I was selected for the USA's World Cup team, but the trip was cancelled. Later, in 1995, I was selected to try out for the US Olympic team in Colorado, but I dislocated my finger on my shooting hand and didn't make the cut. As if that weren't enough, in 1996, I got severe psoriasis, and with that I also got severe arthritis. Only 2% of the world's population get psoriasis, and within that group, only 3% get psoriatic arthritis to go along with it. I hit the jackpot. It was not enough just to get it, but I had to get it severely. Ninety percent of my body was covered with the skin disease, and I had severe swelling in all of my joints, including my jaws. I tried to continue playing ball, but the pain was too much to bear. Plus my skin looked so ugly, and the burning and itching was constant and severe. It got to the point where I was taking up to seven Benadryl tablets every four hours, keeping me in a daze all the time. I couldn't sleep, and my health was failing fast. In short, I was in misery all the time.

But I wasn't about to give up my newfound abilities to be the center of attention, so I took massive amounts of pain killers and antihistamine to keep up my lifestyle. I even turned that life up about ten notches; above all, I had to prove to myself that I could still live it. Along the way, I hurt a lot of people. It amazed me that despite the severity of my illness, I was still able to be such a party man and womanizer. I know that sounds incredible, but I guess people love a confident person, no matter what that person looks like.

Unfortunately, all the medication I was taking caused even more health problems. I had internal bleeding for a long time, and my joints were visibly damaged from the arthritis. And although my confidence enabled me to obtain jobs easily, I couldn't keep them because I was sick all the time. Therefore, I'd lose one job and get another, only to lose it, with the cycle repeating itself over and over again. Life just kept getting worse.

A new purpose

Although it might seem that things were about as bad as they could be, it was at this low point that I first began to get an idea of a larger purpose for my life. During my playing time at UTA, our team was sponsored – and our basketball chairs were provided by – the largest wheelchair manufacturing company in the country. Every time I received a new basketball chair, however, I found that it wasn't built correctly. There were always things that hampered the chair's effectiveness, or that could at least be improved upon. One day, I was so frustrated with the chairs that a teammate of mine, William Hernandez, and I decided we should design our own sports chairs. We put that plan into action, and Willie carried the dream all the way through, creating a custom wheelchair design and manufacturing company called Per4max Medical. It still produces the most elite chairs on the market today, which sell briskly, albeit to an admittedly small market. I became the outside sales rep for Per4max in 2005 and really got to know the business. Again, however, my health held me back. I decided that since health challenges would obviously continue to be part of my life; I might as well accept them and pursue a career which wouldn't be impeded by those challenges. I realized that I needed to start my own business so I could keep a job.

It was then that I got the entrepreneur bug. Ideas started to flow, and it all came together for me in a series of many eureka moments. I had found a purpose; I became passionate about being in a business that assisted the disabled community through products and services that they needed, while at the same time promoting wheelchair sports. My great desire was – and is – to create opportunities for others to enjoy the athletic experiences I have always been fortunate enough to enjoy. And my mission is to offer products, services, and resources; to reach out to the disabled community in order to create and promote those opportunities. That in itself is a pretty big mission, but I didn't want to stop there. I also intend to design the next generation of different price grades of wheelchairs and adaptive sports equipment to better foster my goal of liberating the disabled community. And there is an even greater mission: I want to inspire others, through speaking about my ideas and experiences. I want to help foster in others the self-confidence to say, with conviction: "I can choose whatever life I want for myself – and nothing can stop me."

Today I'm back in Houston, reunited with my family. Besides being involved in my business, I am still very deeply involved in wheelchair sports and am currently the president of the Greater Houston Athletic Association for the Physically Disabled (GHAAPD), a 501C3 non-profit organization (ghaapd.org). I'm also assistant coach of the Houston Challengers' Indoor Wheelchair Soccer team. As I write this, we've captured the National Championship Title for two years in a row. My agenda as president is for huge growth, in order to make a big impact in the community, with the ultimate goal of providing adaptive sports opportunities to all of the Texas Gulf Coast area. I've been working with the University of Houston to push for an Intercollegiate Wheelchair Basketball program, where I hope to be a coach or program director. From there, I hope to work with other local colleges, eventually assisting them in starting their own programs.

Cindy Cline-Flores

Thank you for taking the time to read my story. If there is one message I want to convey, it is this: Choose to have hope, because hope is the one thing that is always real. I think it really is a matter of choice; we truly can choose to live happily. In my case, and the case of many of my people, the choice was clear. Perhaps it's because for us the past is simply incomprehensible, so far beyond any acceptable reality that we can't help but run the other way. Yet the flame of those past torments is always there at arm's length, and we never forget how hot it is. We know better than to touch the flame, because it will burn us. Although I never presume to know what works best for everyone, I believe that the key to a happier life, whether you have survived unspeakable atrocities as my people have, or have grown up among peace and plenty, is this: Don't waste too much time and energy wondering why something happened, or what you could have or should have done to make it turn out differently. You can't control the world outside yourself, nor make the Universe do your bidding. But you can control the world within.

It all comes back down to the fact that you can always make the choice to embrace hope, for that is the one thing that never dies, as long as there is life.

~ *Chhay Mak*

The Boys

Abraham Liberates Abraham

The small East Texas town of Tyler was a place of peace and tranquility during the early years of the twentieth century. It was a good time to be a young boy, and Frank and Buck Abraham took full advantage. They grew up best of friends, inseparable in the adventures of just being boys. As the older of the two, Buck was always watching out for his kid brother.

However, like so many dreams of that gentle time, the days of being "the boys" were shattered with the growing shadow of the war in Europe. It seemed that each day brought the war closer and closer to America, and all too quickly, the shadow loomed, seemingly omnipresent, over the nation's consciousness. It even touched places like Tyler, so long removed from the worries of the larger world.

Just as Buck was graduating from high school, he found himself caught up in the fury of the war, and immediately upon graduating, enlisted in the Air Force to do his part, whatever that was to be. As his life became filled with his flight training, and the war became ever more real to him, his little brother found himself more alone than he had ever been. After two years without his best friend at his side, Frank finally graduated from high school. He immediately enlisted in the army, hoping to both do his part in the struggle that so consumed the world, and to somehow follow Buck into that place that had separated them.

In the spring of 1941, shortly before entering college at The University of Texas, Frank enlisted in the Army Specialized Training Program (ASTP). While the program was supposed to be a year long, Frank ended up being sent to Europe before completing the program because the Army was in desperate need of replacements for servicemen who had been killed in the invasion of Normandy. Like thousands of other young men of the time, he chafed at the seemingly senseless assignments that kept him out of the "real" war. And to make matters even worse, he was struck with devastating news, buried in a list on the back page of his hometown newspaper: Lieutenant Robert S. Abraham – Buck – had been shot down while on a mission over

Hungary. Though the boys' family had known about it for some time, they had refrained from telling Frank, in the hopes of keeping his spirits high by shielding him from the horror of the war in any way they could. They shared the details of family life and good times in Tyler, but figured that Frank had enough to worry about, without getting bad news from home – especially since they had no way of knowing whether Buck was alive or dead, captured by the enemy, or making his way back as best he could.

After parachuting from his damaged aircraft, Buck was captured by the German Volksguard, where he was beaten severely before being turned over to the German SS. Three months later, he was interred in the POW camp in Moosburg, northeast of Munich, Germany, where he would remain for the remainder of his captivity. Buck would often tell the other prisoners, "I'm not worried. My kid brother's in the infantry, and he'll see that we are turned loose." His fellow prisoners must have thought Buck was either really boastful, or just plain crazy. As it turned out, he may well have been a bit psychic.

While Buck was suffering the horrors of life in the prison camp, Frank spent the same two years fighting on the front lines in Europe, experiencing the hell of Remagen Bridge and the Battle of the Bulge. As point man in 1st Company of the Fighting 99th Division, Frank spent one particularly long night crouched in a foxhole, as 88mm shells called "Screamin' Mimis" exploded all around him. It was the start of the Battle of the Bulge, and like most of the troops, Frank found himself making all kinds of promises and deals with God. One such promise he made was to make a difference if God would just let him survive this horrible attack. Throughout the night, bombs screamed overhead and exploded all around his foxhole. The noise alone was enough to drive some men mad, but Frank stayed hunkered down, praying. As the sun began to rise, the shelling stopped, and the blissful quiet returned. Frank looked up to find his foxhole surrounded by huge black craters. On a night that so many had perished, Frank's prayers had been answered. He had survived.

A few weeks later, Frank was summoned to company headquarters, where he was ordered to report to command headquarters. He was informed that his colonel, who knew that Frank's brother was interred in one of the camps, had reassigned him to the G2 service, with new duties that included scouting out POW camps and liberating prisoners. Frank traveled across Europe from camp to camp, releasing prisoners and seeing to their welfare. Wherever he went, he always asked about his big brother. He would often commandeer Jeeps on his off time to search area camps, in the chance that he might find Buck. While on one of these missions, Frank heard about a camp that was thought to hold over 14,000

Cindy Cline-Flores

prisoners and forced laborers. He made his way to the camp, and was greeted warmly by the throngs of prisoners as he drove down the camp's main drive. As Buck tells the story, he saw a Jeep coming down the street and said to a fellow prisoner, "Hey… that fellow in the Jeep looks just like my baby brother Frank." Of course, Buck's fellow prisoners had long ago grown accustomed to his promise that his little brother would save them, and probably just nodded their heads, humoring his fantasy. One can only imagine what went through their minds when Frank actually pulled up, saw Buck, and jumped out of the Jeep. By the time the brothers embraced, laughed, shook hands, cried, and embraced again, the other men had become believers!

After the excitement and fuss of their unlikely reunion had died down a bit, Frank made arrangements for Buck to have a decent meal and a bed to sleep in for the night – the first he had experienced in two years. Shortly thereafter, Buck was on his way home. In a letter home to his parents, Frank wrote:

1 May 1945

Dear Mother and Dad,

Just a NEWS FLASH – Abraham Liberated Abraham. Col. St. Clair took me down and I went out to the camp and LIBERATED the kid. Oh Happy Day – It was wonderful. We spent the night just shooting the bull. He's fine, and I will write all the details tomorrow. Hope he doesn't beat this letter home. You should have seen Buckie. Life was truly just a bowl of cherries.

Signed "The Liberator," Frank

While Buck's version of the story is full of colloquialisms and East Texas color, Frank's is more sedate and humble. I have no doubt that both are equally true from each of their perspectives. The details are not nearly as important as the fact that these two brothers loved and admired each other. What is amazing is that "The Boys" found each other, half way around the world, at a time when the world was still a huge place, and when mere survival was a major accomplishment.

This story of liberation shows how each brother – facing adversity – overcame and survived, but it doesn't end there. In fact, it is just the beginning of a more important story; of keeping promises and making a difference. Buck came home and lived a full life, raising a family and operating a successful business. Frank went back to school and graduated from The University of Texas Law School. He moved to Houston and began working for one of the city's largest litigation firms. A few years later he started a firm of his own that ultimately became one of the city's leading firms. He married Nancy, and got on with the process of raising a family.

But the promises he had made that hellish night in the foxhole stayed with Frank. He had made a vow to make a difference, and for the remainder of his life, Frank did make a difference, one life at a time. Frank believed in many things, including a good education. He believed that if you reached kids at an early age, educated them, gave them the tools for success, and taught them tolerance and acceptance, they could change the world. With these simple ideas, Frank had begun working with kids through Big Brothers. In 1972, he was even named Big Brother of the Year by the National Association. He eventually moved on to form his own foundation, which he called the Abraham Student Aid Foundation, to assist students with tuition and books. A few years later, he shortened the name of the association to Student Aid Foundation Enterprises (SAFE). In 1999, Frank began a program called Peace by Piece, which brought students from around the globe to Unity World Headquarters in Lee's Summit, Missouri, where they spent two weeks each summer interacting with each other. They learned about the beauty of diversity, religious tolerance, and social responsibility, and were taught how to share what they learned with their peers in their own communities. Frank sent the group's leadership to the United Nations to address the delegates on the need for peace and acceptance. He also sent the group to The University for Peace outside of San Jose, Costa Rica. Working with Dr. Robert Muller, former Assistant Secretary General to the United Nations, the students were given leadership training on world peace, based on a world core curriculum.

Frank has truly kept the promise he made that night, a lifetime ago. He once humbly stated that he didn't really feel like he had done enough, or that he had fallen short at times. But just ask one of his students, one of his torch-bearers for peace. One good example is a young man who was about to enter high school in Costa Rica. Frank met him at a social gathering one Saturday night, and after they talked for just a short time, Frank invited the boy to come to the United States to attend high

Cindy Cline-Flores

school and college, with Frank paying all his expenses. On that Sunday evening, the boy began a life-altering journey as he accompanied Frank and Nancy back to Houston.

Over the years, the number of children whose lives have been affected by Frank are countless. The lessons they learned because of his promise will affect generations to come. The kids called him Father Abraham, and they knew he always kept his promise. And just as Abraham had liberated Abraham so many years ago, Frank found true riches by bringing that liberation to others throughout the course of his life.

~ Cindy Cline-Flores

Myra Jolivet, with her children, Shelby and Samuel Washington
Photo by Alisa Murray

Cindy Cline-Flores

Accepting The Presence
Finding The Power

No one plans to spend fourteen years enmeshed in a child custody battle. It just happens. And when a case drags on for such a long time, it inevitably becomes rife with angst and acrimony. Mine was all that and more. Add to that some of the other aspects of my life, like having no immediate family living anywhere nearby, a television contract gone sour, and the death of my father in California, and it seemed that the whole world had conspired to take me to the brink of emotional and financial ruin.

When I first got married, I didn't know that men hit women. It was not in my history, and definitely never happened with my parents. It wasn't too long after the wedding, however, that I began to learn just how sheltered I had been. By the time my husband struck me for the third time, I knew for certain that he was not my true life partner, and that the home life we had together was not what I wanted for my children, ages ten months and three years. I did the only thing I felt I could do: I ran. I left a beautiful home and all of the trappings of an outwardly wonderful life to be safe near my immediate family in California. My intent was to move West, get a job, and begin making a new life for myself and my children. When I arrived in California, however, I learned that my father was dying. Between the situation I had left behind in Texas and coming face to face with my father's impending death, I was so fragile and traumatized that I did very poorly in the job interviews I went on.

I cannot blame employers for not hiring me; I probably wouldn't have hired me, either. As a result, I remained unemployed for some time, dependent upon friends for our most basic needs. While we always had food, shelter, and transportation – and sympathetic shoulders to cry upon – I was not, according to my ex-husband's lawyers, providing a suitable environment for my children. Ultimately, he convinced a judge that the children would be better provided for in his home, and he took the opportunity to legally take my babies from me. I knew immediately that I had to return to Texas to try and get them back.

I had no idea what I was up against, as I was completely unfamiliar with the family court process. By all superficial accounts, I had the disadvantage of being an unemployed former TV personality, born and bred in the notoriously unconventional Berkeley, California area. Even my Louisiana roots did little to bolster my image as a "normal" mother in the judge's eyes. I learned very quickly how difficult it can be to convince strangers that you live every moment of your life devoted to the well-being of your children. I tried to help them see how ludicrous it was for my ex to claim that he was a good and loving parent to the children, when his actions toward their mother were hurtful and hateful.

In an early hearing, the judge laid out the challenge I faced. If I wanted my children, I had to find a good-paying job and a home, and show that I could keep the children in a manner close to what they had known before the divorce. Since I had no job, no place of my own to live, and no hope, my ex seemed to hold all the cards. After all, he still held a long-time corporate position, was easily able to pay for the house, and had three lawyers fighting for him.

I so clearly remember lying awake at two o'clock one morning, heaving and wailing with grief and fear, when an incredible Guiding Spirit spoke to me in the heart-language that was clear and unmistakable. It was the first time I actually had the sensation of a real voice speaking to me!

That sweet voice said, "Everything will be all right." It was calm, genderless, and firm. I couldn't help but wonder if the voice knew how bad my situation really was. After all, I was penniless, had no job prospects, and was thoroughly drained after fighting so hard to keep my two toddlers. But somewhere inside, I knew that the voice was right, and that the burdens I was carrying would eventually be eased. A sense of peace such as I had not known for a long time – if ever – washed over me, and I stopped crying.

Literally days before my next big court hearing, I was hired by Mayor Kathy Whitmire. I tried to tell her that I was too damaged to be a good addition to her office, but she believed in me. When opposing counsel asked if I even had a job, I was able to tell them that I had accepted a position with the mayor's office. As if a floodgate had been opened, other blessings began to roll in miraculously, as big and proud as that new job!

From that moment on, I realized the difference between circumstances and reality. I later learned the term, 'breakdown before breakthrough,' and thought it must have been coined especially for me.

Before it was all over, I had lost everything but my children. I... no, *we*, started over, literally from scratch, and have reaped abundantly. We have shared big and been blessed big. This is not to suggest that challenges do not

Cindy Cline-Flores

continue to find their way into my heart, mind, or door. Nowadays, however, they reach a much stronger adversary – one fortified by an ever-growing understanding of and trust in Divine wisdom and order.

It is true; there is a Presence and a Power, urging us to seek and find our Divine plan. It often waits just around the corner from 'ruin,' and inches away from 'continued blessing!'

~ *Myra Jolivet*

Ticynn London
Photo by Alisa Murray

Cindy Cline-Flores

Celebrate Life

When Mike and Regina London admitted their four-year-old daughter, Ticynn, to the hospital early in 2000, they were not prepared for bad news. Ticynn had a flu-like virus that had her parents and doctors puzzled, but what she also had was much worse than the flu: doctors at Boston Children's Hospital discovered she had fanconi anemia, or FA. An inherited anemia caused by a gene in one or both parents, FA is found typically in children. It is considered to be a blood disease, but can affect all systems of the body and, because it leads to bone marrow failure, it is often fatal. The bad news was that even after bone-marrow transplants, victims are highly susceptible to cancer. But a transplant seemed to be Ticynn's only hope.

Mike London, who at this writing is an assistant coach with the Houston Texans, was living in Virginia with Regina and the couple's four children when Ticynn was first diagnosed. Mike went through the roller coaster of emotions faced by all parents with a critically ill child. He suffered the profound guilt; he and Regina had never even heard of FA, let alone known they were carrying the gene for this potentially fatal disorder. He went through the endless questioning – "Why me? Why my daughter?" And he felt the desperate surge of hope as the search for a donor began.

The odds were stacked against Ticynn. Because she was African American and because she was so young, the chances of finding a donor other than a sibling were very slim. Unfortunately, her three younger siblings were not suitable. Her mother Regina was tested and found not to be suitable either – which was not surprising, because the odds that either of her parents would match were ten thousand to one.

That's why the doctors were shocked when they discovered that Mike London's bone marrow was a perfect match.

It was then that Mike experienced his first wave of hope. Knowing he was literally his daughter's only chance, he prayed that he was, for lack of a better word, worthy, that the lifestyle he had led up to that point would make him "acceptable to being a donor," as he put it. He did not allow himself to go to that dark place of wondering what the family would have done if he hadn't been a match. He was determined to look ahead with hope, however tenuous that hope might be.

Being young, resilient, and otherwise healthy, Ticynn recovered from the virus for which she had initially been hospitalized. Her blood-cell counts were stable, and Mike and Regina were told that a bone-marrow transplant could wait one year, or perhaps even up to five years. However, Ticynn was to have monthly checkups to have her blood counts taken, and these were to continue up until the time of the transplant, whenever that might be.

And so began the wait. Mike and Regina knew that every day they had with their daughter was a gift, and both were also deeply and constantly aware of the responsibility that had been placed on Mike's shoulders. Regina discouraged Mike from any risky activity – "no riding motorcycles, no doing this, no doing that," she told a reporter. They even asked the doctors about what could be done if the unthinkable happened; if Mike were to die, would there be a way to keep him alive long enough to get the bone marrow? Not that they were anticipating such an occurrence, but since Mike was the only possible match for their daughter, they felt they had to consider all possibilities.

In the spring of 2003, Ticynn was still healthy, but it had become apparent that a transplant would be needed within a year. The Johns Hopkins Hospital in Baltimore has one of the most prestigious transplant centers in the country, and it was only a three-hour drive from the University of Virginia, where Mike had accepted a job. That was where Ticynn's transplant would take place.

On April 23, she was admitted to Johns Hopkins to begin chemotherapy and radiation. By April 24, her own bone marrow was all gone, and she still faced several long days of treatment in preparation for the transplant. Mike continued working right up to the day when he arrived at the hospital to have his bone marrow removed. During the time Ticynn was hospitalized, Mike drove many times between the family's home in Charlottesville, Virginia and Baltimore. It was during this long drive that the tears would flow, sometimes developing into uncontrollable sobs. Most of the time Mike was okay, but when the emotions hit, they hit hard. But he kept his tears hidden from his daughter, and by the time he arrived at Johns Hopkins he had managed to put on a face of encouragement for her, since he knew that she needed his strength and reassurance as desperately as she needed his bone marrow.

On April 28, Ticynn's last day of chemo and radiation, Mike London made that long drive to the hospital to have his own marrow drawn, a two-hour procedure. By this time, Ticynn was very weak, her bone marrow count at zero. There was nothing for her to do but lie there and wait for "my daddy's blood," as she put it – a gift he joyfully gave.

And then came the day of reckoning: April 29, 2003.

Mike and Regina sat together next to Ticynn's hospital bed, watching while doctors connected a small bag of Mike's bone marrow to Ticynn's IV. The seven-year-old was sound asleep, exhausted and weak after six days of chemo and radiation. The Londons watched as the bone marrow entered Ticynn's body, drip by drip. It seemed to take forever, but it really only took half an hour. After being consumed by their three-year wait, the parents were nearly as exhausted as their daughter.

The moment the transplant was complete, Ticynn popped up in bed. Regina and Mike panicked, fearing she was having some bad reaction to the bone marrow. Instead she sat up straight and looked around the room, and then asked when the transplant was going to start.

The relief her parents felt was palpable.

Doctors, too, were amazed by how rapidly the little girl's body had accepted the bone marrow, and everybody was astounded by her positive attitude. Even when her lovely long hair began falling out soon after the transplant, Ticynn was unfazed. As larger and larger clumps began to fall out, Ticynn finally said, "Mom, let's just shave it off." In fact, Regina was more upset about the hair than her daughter was. "When her hair came out, that's when the reality of everything hit me," Regina said.

Mike, meanwhile, was worn out, still making those trips between Charlottesville and Baltimore to see his daughter, but trying to spend as much time as possible with the couple's other children, as well as doing his recruiting job for the University of Virginia. It distressed him that he couldn't be with Ticynn more, but he tried to maintain a steady calm and a balance in his life.

And there was a lot to be thankful for. Soon after the transplant, Ticynn's blood-cell counts started rising, doubling and then tripling. Doctors – you know, those people who are normally given to medical mumbo-jumbo – repeatedly used the word "miracle" when talking about Ticynn. On May 19, she was discharged from Johns Hopkins and moved into a hospital closer to home to complete her recovery. In July, the family received the wonderful news that Ticynn could go home, six weeks earlier than expected.

She was not out of the woods yet, however. The doctors warned that she would have to be carefully watched, because for one year there was a chance her body could reject the transplant. So the family immediately changed their lifestyle. Their daughter couldn't be in large crowds, couldn't go to school, and had to wear a face mask, even for a quick public outing.

Despite these restrictions, Ticynn plowed on, continuing to stun doctors with her recovery. By October of 2003, the central line inserted into her chest for daily doses of medication was removed. On October 29, she passed the six-month mark, and there were still no problems. And then in January, she defied the odds again when her doctors said she was well enough to return to school.

There were still restrictions, of course; if a classmate sneezed or coughed excessively, she had to place a mask over her face. And she still had to avoid large crowds and strange environments, which meant that assemblies and field trips were out.

Finally April 29, 2004 came around – the one-year anniversary of Ticynn's transplant. On that day, she threw her masks into the garbage, and the entire London family celebrated what they call her "New Life Birthday." They made a pact to celebrate that birthday every year, and it's a pact they have gladly kept.

When Mike was offered his first job in the NFL, the Londons felt it was meant to be. Reliant Stadium, home of the Houston Texans, is less than a mile from the world-renowned Texas Medical Center, a fact that was nearly as appealing as the job itself. So the family packed up and headed to the Bayou City, where Mike coaches the defensive line for the Texans.

As for Ticynn, she would much rather be playing soccer or swimming than sitting in on a Texans' practice session. But there's no denying she is grateful for the gift of life her father gave her. And as for Mike... well, he finds it hard to talk about his daughter without tears welling up, tears for which he makes no apologies. He says that when you look at her, you look at life, at a gift that was given to her through him. Much more so than is the case with most parents and children, she is literally a part of him, as he is of her.

"I celebrate life every day now," Mike says. And he is grateful, so profoundly grateful, that his family – including the daughter he very nearly lost – is there to celebrate it with him.

~ *Cindy Cline-Flores*

Lori Considine
Photo by Alisa Murray

Cindy Cline-Flores

An Intentional Creation

If you could just count to three and close your eyes and die without pain and effortlessly slip from this world into heaven, would you do it? This was the question I asked and answered in my high school English class, thinking that surely there would be supporters of my idea. There were none. Not only that, but my teacher got this tragically worried look on her face, and I'm pretty sure she was wrestling with the idea of running to the counselors' office for immediate advice. But just as quickly as she seemed to have lost composure, she managed to find it again and proceed with class as if there had not been a giant elephant standing among us waiting for validation. I had told dozens of people my 1-2-3 theory and not one seemed alarmed enough to probe for more thoughts on the subject.

I played the perfect child, and whenever my mother asked if anything was wrong, I denied having any real issues to deal with, but the reality was that at some point I stopped pretending that everything was fine, and stopped denying my inner turmoil. I gave into my thoughts about suicide and began a non-stop campaign to end my life.

As a teenager, when I felt like the pressure of my life was bigger than my ability to cope with it, I would resort to cutting. I primarily focused on my wrists because that's what Molly Ringwald did in a movie I saw, and I was too naïve to think of something original. I doubt it was the intention of the producer to glamorize suicide and cutting, but for me that's exactly what happened. Before watching the movie, I just knew I was sad and frustrated, but after the movie I was actually excited about having found a viable outlet for the thoughts and feelings I was having. It was the height of the eighties, when Cyndi Lauper and Madonna were dictating the fashions of the world, so I adopted my own twisted fashion by combining my preppie alligator shirts with matching bandanas wrapped around my wrists. I was so sure it was obvious that I was crumbling under the weight of my world that I believed the reason no one asked about my new fashion statement was not because they didn't notice, but because they didn't care. I used that insecurity as the rocket that launched my campaign to end my life to the next level.

Throughout high school I vacillated between thinking I could overcome my sinking feeling and fearing it would drown me. I not only had suicidal tendencies like cutting, but I purposely went out of my way to put myself in gravely dangerous situations, such as boldly going to seedy places unescorted, or using my car to aggressively catapult a sense of thrill into my life. I made many bad choices during those days, which worked to exacerbate the problem. I do not believe that my attempts at suicide were nothing more than a crazy way of trying to garner attention. Too many people make the assumption that suicidal persons are merely looking for attention, and in my opinion, based upon my own experiences, that isn't always so. It depends upon the person, but if anyone in your life is talking of suicide or acting in self-destructive ways, or if you are having suicidal tendencies yourself, please seek help. I can't stress that enough. Even if the suicide attempts are "merely" a bid for attention, they indicate that something is very wrong in the person's life and needs to be addressed.

In my own case, I truly wanted to die, and I was very nearly successful in my attempt to end my life. I was convinced that life was pointless and that I would never be able to overcome the hurdles I believed I would need to clear in order to move forward in my life. So why not just check out early and wake up in Heaven? For me, checking out early wasn't some big plan to call attention to myself; it was a simple, quiet plan to escape my reality and wake up in a perfect place. I just wanted to forget the things I had allowed to cloud my life. I wanted to start over, and I just couldn't see how that would ever be possible in a human world.

By age eighteen, my reckless behavior and attempts at suicide landed me in a padded cell in a straitjacket, with my arms bandaged from my wrists to my elbows, feeling the pain of 69 stitches and staples that held the skin of my arms together. I had no place else to look but up.

Looking back on my time spent in the psych ward following my most serious suicide attempt, I realize that it gave me the insight that would later help me save others' lives as a 911 emergency operator and suicide interventionist. Of course I took the state-mandated courses that teach you how to talk someone off a ledge or away from the productive end of a bullet, but I also had firsthand insight into the emotions and the feelings of people who so desperately wanted to end their own lives. It was my own personal experience that aided me in talking Robert off the balcony of his hotel room. Had it not been for the past anguish in my own life, I would not have gained the respect of Leon, who let me talk him into giving his gun to the officer outside his door before he shot his head off. I would not have been able to guide Taylor away from her own thoughts of suicide when her desperate mom came to me for help. I never would have been in a position to go in and pray with Jose for peace and guidance when he blew half his face away in an attempt to end his life. Jose never would have let me in his room for that prayer had I not first shown him my own scars.

You are not a bad person, or crazy, or weak, or flawed, because you feel suicidal. It doesn't necessarily even mean that you really want to die – it only means that you have reached the point where it is absolutely necessary to devise a plan to reclaim your happiness. And willpower has nothing to do with it. Nor does the fact that someone thinks your problems are nothing compared to the "real" problems in the world. Don't ever accept it if someone tells you that whatever is causing you pain is "not enough to be suicidal about." No one is the keeper of your emotions but you.

Despite my own desperate attempts to end my life, it became perfectly clear to me that God had a plan for my life, and that it was not up to me to determine when it might end or how. I believe that part of God's plan for me is to reach out to others and help save their lives, and help them to reclaim their hope in life.

My turning point came one Sunday when, through a series of uncommon events, I ended up at a church I had never been to before (or since). I will never forget what the speaker said about why we are all here. Here is the essence of the message:

"You did not come into this world because your parents met and fell in love and decided to have a baby. You were not the accidental by-product of teenagers in love, and you were not manufactured at a baby farm by a mad scientist. Before you were born, God looked out across the world and saw a need for you. God weighed the logistics and viewed them from every angle, and as far back as your parents, grandparents, and their parents' grandparents, God began to make a path by which He would bring you into the world – right down to the minute details of what experiences your parents would endure as children that would cause them to be the kind of people that would influence you to be the person He created you to be, and to live the life that is best able to reflect His love and spur you to worship."

After I heard that message, I began to look at my life in an entirely new way. I came to understand that it is not my parents' "fault" that I am here. I was chosen by God, created by His hand, and He knew me even before I was conceived. (Jeremiah 1:5) I now believe I was *chosen* by God to live. It was the dawn of a new season of my life, knowing I was not a fluke, an accident or the product of selfish ambition by my parents to form a family. I am an intentional creation, made with a purpose – and God loved me, specifically me.

For me, the answers I needed came from the Bible. The Bible says we are to humble ourselves as servants and we will be fulfilled. Over the years I learned just how true that really was. I've found that the more I serve others, the more important and loved I feel.

When I survey the peaks and valleys of my life and picture it in my mind as a chart or graph, it is easy to see the times when I let my own stubbornness and rebellion dictate my life and cause myself turmoil. When I actively seek the will of God to direct me along the paths that lead to still waters, I'm able to begin to live a life blessed by God, a life where happiness prevails, a life where there is always hope.

Psalm 39:7 "But now, Lord, what do I look for? My hope is in you."

~Lori Considine

Elizabeth McIngvale
Photo by Alisa Murray

Cindy Cline-Flores

Life With OCD

hen I was a little girl, I was, for the most part, pretty happy. I had parents who loved me and saw to it that I didn't want for anything, and good friends to whom I could always turn when facing what passes for a crisis in a young girl's mind. Then, at the age of twelve, my life quickly turned into a horrible nightmare. Where I had previously taken some pride in the way I looked and acted, something happened inside me that turned my earlier efforts into an all-consuming series of bizarre rituals that soon took over my life.

I had always been the kind of girl who wanted to stay neat and clean, but by the time I was twelve, it got to the point where no amount of washing and scrubbing was enough, and I quickly ended up with hands that were dry, cracked, and bleeding. No matter how much I tried, I just couldn't stop. It seemed like I could never walk away from the sink. I really felt like I was stuck and had no way out. I knew intellectually that my actions made no sense, but that knowledge couldn't overcome my need to continue cleaning myself.

I would suddenly become overwhelmed with intrusive thoughts that I had to do these weird things, and the actions became rituals that were, for me, as essential as the very act of breathing. What began with obsessive washing soon turned into obsessive everything. When I would come home, I would lock the door behind me, but that wasn't enough to satisfy my need to keep our home safe. I would check and re-check the locks. Not just one time, but over and over again, ultimately determining that I had to check it forty-two times before I would be certain that I had indeed locked the door! In order to ensure that I had unplugged my hair dryer or turned other electronic devices off, I would repeat the motions – again, forty-two times. I was deathly afraid that if I didn't turn them off according to the ritual I had come up with, my family's house might burn down and it would be all my fault. I started retracing my steps, endlessly repeating virtually every move that I made. I feared that if I crossed over a crack in the sidewalk or seam in the floor with a bad thought in mind, whatever that thought might be would come true, and something bad would happen. Again, it would be my fault. No matter how much I would try to reason with myself and tell myself that I couldn't cause the kinds of calamities I imagined, reason simply couldn't overcome the fear – and the tremendous burden of responsibility and guilt – that I felt. It would take me hours at times to get from my bed to the back door, simply because it never felt right. I would miss performing one of my rituals (or just not know for certain that I had performed them correctly), and have to go back to where I started and begin all over again. I knew that it didn't make sense, and that my fears would not really come true, but I could not stop. I was trapped, living in this horrific nightmare.

As I continued to do these rituals, I tried my best to hide what was going on. When my hands were cracking and bleeding I told my mom that I had an allergic reaction to the soap, in hopes that she wouldn't realize what was really going on. I was so deeply scared all the time, and although I knew the things I was doing didn't make sense, I was certain that no one else would understand the sense of foreboding I felt. Their reassurances certainly couldn't make me feel safe.

I lived this nightmare alone, in secret, for as long as I could. I tried to keep the thoughts to myself, and tried my best to not do my rituals around my family and friends. But eventually, it got to the point where I just couldn't hide it any more. I broke down and let my mom into this scary, unknown world in which I was living. At first, I didn't tell her about my fears or how desperately I needed to do my rituals. I began to ask her various questions to get reassurance from her that no one was mad at me and that I hadn't done anything wrong. One question quickly turned into twenty, and then one hundred, and so on. I couldn't stop at one question, and soon I was consuming her days with questions and phone calls, making sure she was okay and safe, and ensuring that others were as well. I started to lose weight, and within months, my "normal" life had come to a standstill, replaced with the endless procession of bizarre behaviors that seemed to grow more prevalent every day. Even my most basic ability to function in school became nearly impossible, as were the rest of my typical daily activities such as showering or even walking. I was taking hours in the shower, stuck in the pattern of ritualizing and washing, until the water turned cold, leaving me crying and exhausted. My mom would have to help me get out and get dressed. I literally went from being a functioning teenager to being like a helpless child who needed assistance in my every move. I was lost and confused. My mom's life could no longer be about tending to her business and family, for she was all but consumed with taking care of me.

As my symptoms progressed, my mom knew that I needed help. As much as she tried to understand what was going on with me, it was beyond anything she was prepared for. As a mother, she wanted to do anything that she could to help make my days easier, but her search for answers and conclusions was fruitless. We soon both agreed that I needed help, and I agreed to go see a therapist. After bouncing around from one therapist to another in the Houston area, we finally learned that

Cindy Cline-Flores

I was living with Obsessive Compulsive Disorder (OCD), an anxiety disorder characterized by recurrent, unwanted thoughts (obsessions) and/or repetitive behaviors (compulsions). As comforting as it was to know that there was a name for my struggles (and that I wasn't the only one to be suffering like I was), it was at the same time discouraging, because every therapist we saw told us that my case was the worst they had ever seen, and that it was probably too severe to be treated successfully. However, as my dad always says, we are a family that always fights and doesn't give up. With that in mind, my parents were determined to find help for me, and to find a way for me to regain the life that I once had.

Two days after my fifteenth birthday, my parents took me to the Menninger clinic, located in Topeka, Kansas. The clinic had an inpatient center for adults and adolescents living with Obsessive Compulsive Disorder, and claimed to have a good success rate in treating patients with the affliction. The day we got there was the scariest day of my life. My family was leaving me in a place where I knew no one, and where I would have to directly face my greatest fears on a daily basis. I would have to do those things that caused me the greatest amount of anxiety, and I wasn't so sure that I was ready. At the same time, however, I knew that I was ready to get back home to my life with my family and friends. Holding that goal foremost in my mind, within a few days, I was actively participating in what they referred to as exposure therapy. What that entailed was my being told to imagine a situation that would cause me to feel fearful or anxious, and to delve into those feelings on a deeper and deeper level, until the anxiety would begin to decrease. Sometimes, a session would be very gentle (referred to as systematic desensitization), while at other times, it would feel like every fear I had was being thrown at me all at once (referred to as flooding). It was hard and challenging work. It was exhausting, and many times I felt like it was more than I could handle. At those times, I would remember what my parents always taught me, "If it is to be, it is up to me," and I would continue despite my fears. I continued the treatment, working as hard as I possibly could to reclaim the kind of life I wanted so badly. Three months later, I was told by my therapist that I had made wonderful progress, and was ready to leave the clinic and go home! The day that I left was an emotional day for me, filled with a sense of pride for having come so far, yet tinged with a sense of deep sadness, as well. I had become extremely close to the doctors and other patients, and I hated knowing that I would likely never see any of them again. Just as I had cried the day that I arrived in Topeka, I cried the day that I left. They had given me my life back and had taught me how to fight my OCD every day of my life. It's a battle that I will always face, but thanks to the support of my family, my friends at Menninger, and a deep-seated faith in a loving God, it is a battle that I know I can win.

I know in my heart that there is a reason for everything we experience. Today, at age twenty-two, I believe that I went through the horror of OCD so that I could help others who are afflicted. I am now working on my Masters Degree in order to be able to do for others what doctors and therapists have done for me. I want to work with those living with OCD, to help them regain the lives that they deserve to have. I am the initial national spokesperson for the Obsessive Compulsive Foundation, an organization devoted to helping others understand that they are not alone and that there is help – and hope – for them. In addition, my family and I have started our own nonprofit organization, The Peace of Mind Foundation, to offer support and fund research and treatment for others living with OCD.

This has been a journey that has been trying, difficult, and life altering, but is one that I have never had to fight alone. Although I may have felt alone and scared at times, I always had God by my side, walking with me and guiding me along the path. Even at my lowest point, some part of me knew that God would give me the strength that I needed to fight my OCD, and to continue to do His work. Once I became consciously aware of His presence in my life, I was filled with a hope that was powerful enough to overcome my fear. I have come to think of my life as a blessed journey. Because of (rather than in spite of) what I have been through, I have been able to see God's infinite, loving presence, and to understand that this is my path. It is my turn to inspire others by sharing the story of my life, and to work to provide them with the resources they need in order to overcome their battles with OCD.

I still live with OCD, and will for the rest of my life. I still struggle on a daily basis, but my unbending faith in God is a daily reminder to never give up. No matter how big the battle, we can always face it, for God is always by our side, walking with us. We are never alone, and there is always reason to hope.

~ *Elizabeth McIngvale*

RaNelle Wallace
Photo by Alisa Murray

Cindy Cline-Flores

The Burning Within

Life is like a dream. How often we have all heard that old saying, but there is so much truth in it. Storms and blizzards hit. They come and they go. They are small, medium, big… at times lasting for a night, and at times for what seems a lifetime. But they pass! And there, in the light of love and faith, is left a core of brilliant sunshine, transforming everything in its wake. I know, because I lived that "dream."

Have you ever had a terrible foreboding of something about to happen? A feeling that burned deep within your soul, a feeling of impending danger… but you continued with your plan anyway, though warned repeatedly in dreams, and by others, of misfortune about to happen?

That happened to me. I am RaNelle Wallace, and this is my story of "trial by fire." It is the story of having all I'd worked for snatched away and destroyed, and yet somehow finding the strength within to rise above everything and succeed.

In 1985 I was a beautiful young woman with a career in television, a home, children, and a rocky seven-year marriage. And I lost it all, in a matter of moments, in the blaze of a horrifying fiery plane crash somewhere in the Wasatch Mountains near Fillmore, Utah.

My husband, Terry, and I had taken a trip to Salt Lake City in a last-ditch effort to save our crumbling marriage. That day, having firmly concluded we had no future together, we prepared to fly our single-engine plane home to California in order to file for divorce.

Despite strong and disturbing premonitions of danger, I shrugged off my fears and boarded the plane. A short time later, the small craft flew into a mountainous snowstorm and, after a heart-stopping ride, Terry somehow managed to make an emergency landing in Delta, Utah – about 100 miles from Salt Lake.

Convinced we had been saved by a miracle, I refused to get on the plane again and insisted we finish the trip by car. When Terry learned no rentals were available in that obscure town, he talked me into flying again, stating it was only a fifteen-minute flight into the next town and adding, "What could happen in fifteen minutes?"

Once more ignoring the overwhelming feeling of foreboding, I climbed aboard the plane, this time flying head-on into a nightmare. We soon found ourselves on an even more terrifying ride, battling disorienting wintry weather conditions. Our vulnerable aircraft crashed into the side of a mountain, and was instantaneously transformed into a raging inferno. After struggling with the towering flames, Terry emerged miraculously unscathed, but I suffered severe disfiguring burns that would never leave me the same.

With over 75% of my body charred and in severe pain, I struggled for my life as I inched down a jagged and treacherous mountainside seeking help. After reaching the freeway, nearly five and a half miles down the base of the mountain, and having given all I had within to give, I finally let go of life when a paramedic told me, "Stop fighting; we'll do all the work for you."

In that instant I found myself leaving this world of suffering and pain, to arrive in a new realm of absolute peace and profound love. While in those celestial havens, I was pronounced clinically brain dead, and literally heard the doctors order the nurse to find a relative who could sign a release for my organs. And yet with a tube in my throat, and wires and hoses protruding from my arms, I was somehow able to communicate with a special nurse who also truly felt that "burning within" – a burning to keep on fighting rather than giving up. Even to this day, only a few people know of the sacrifices made behind the security-guarded doors of that hospital burn unit, by both patients and staff, to bring me back to life.

But bring me back to life they did. My story was far from over.

Just hours after being released from the hospital, I confronted my worst fear – to be seen in public wearing a Jobst mask, complete with plastic protrusions. I was stopped by suspicious guards at the airport – in front of my children – merely because of the fear my face caused. Some months later, I was even arrested for the same reason.

Then one morning just two months following my hospital release, while healing at home, I glanced out my bedroom window across a spacious field to behold the unimaginable – my neighbor's home had flames leaping from the roof! Barely dressed, and with open wounds from my unhealed burns, I instinctively sprang from the bedroom, dashed out the front door and raced across the three empty lots to reach the fiery house.

The scenario was like that of the plane crash – the gray and foggy weather, the ground, and the flames. Yet there was a burning within as well, and it was fueled by a powerful feeling that someone inside was still asleep. So I entered the blazing garage, and suddenly found myself trapped inside the inferno as the automatic garage door closed behind me.

I was forced to face the merciless flames that had robbed me of my face, my beauty, my skin, and the life I once had. Up to that moment I had not even been able to sit near a fireplace or cook on the stove because of the overwhelming fear left within me from the accident. In that trapped space, I nearly gave in to my fate… ready to let the fire take me away… But the burning within proved far more powerful than the flames around me. At once I experienced myself kicking and banging on the door and the cars in a desperate attempt to awaken anyone who might be inside. And with one sure kick, the garage door opened – just wide enough for me to slide out.

Frantically I ran around to the front door, meeting a woman who was emerging from the smoke-filled house. Though she screamed from the sight of my open wounds, she immediately realized the danger she and her loved ones were in. Together we went in that house and rescued the two young girls who still lay sleeping. As they huddled on the lawn in front of the burning house comforting one another, I realized what I had just accomplished – and learned – by facing my worst nightmarish fear.

Following that triumph, my life changed quickly and dramatically. I had acted out of instinct, and to me my act was only human, but others considered me to be a hero, and news of my heroism was published around the world. Newsweek magazine featured the story in a special issue of "America's Greatest Heroes." Overnight I became a local celebrity, and reports of the living hell I had suffered became the talk of the town. Although I did not seek this attention, it turned out to be a true blessing. As people began to hear and read about my story, a rallying cry went out to help secure for me the medical attention I desperately needed. Doctors offered services, and fund raisers were organized, but still the money could not cover the exorbitant costs of my multiple surgeries. My family was bankrupt.

Still I did not give up, and after months of mental and physical rehabilitation, I felt a keen desire welling up within to do something for others. I began actively teaching children and others about fire safety and burn awareness, and counseled many on how to overcome adversity. Even psychologists sought my guidance and help.

As the news spread about my service and work, I was chosen by the California legislature to receive the Woman of the Year Award, leading many people to encourage me to run for the office of Mayor of Bakersfield, California. I accepted the challenge. I was only 26, contending against the "good old boys" who spent over $50,000, only to win a narrow victory. My $160 budget still holds the county record for the most votes won per dollar. The experience and insight of politics taught me how to get things accomplished in the world around me, but most of all I learned to never, ever give up!

Though I vigilantly projected an attitude of success over the years following the accident, my body eventually began to fail. I was diagnosed with a rare form of cancer in 1997 and was told that, barring an act of God, I would never have any more children. More surgeries took a toll on my well-being, and my marriage was again on the rocks. The walls were crumbling in. Since then I have endured the loss of that marriage, my father's death, a daughter-in-law who nearly lost her life – along with my first-born grandchild – to cancer during her pregnancy, and I became a key witness in a murder trial.

It was at this point in my life that I dug deep inside to ask myself a long awaited question: Why had I returned to this world after beholding the glories of the next? It was then that I found the answer.

Our purpose in life is to share our experiences in a manner that helps those around us who are suffering from discouragement, depression, and despair. These sufferers are everywhere, and if our hands do not reach out to them, our experience in life is vain. When others are hit by the "cold fires" of life hurled by the hands of fate, we are the hands of love that can help heal them, returning them to the "warm fires" of caring hearts.

I continue on through life to overcome adversities and find joy in living every day, to pass through life's storms and into the brilliance of the sunlight that shines through when those storms pass. Today, I am a successful author and presenter, and I share my experiences with gratitude to all who will hear. Through my own journey, I have seen how one can miraculously overcome even the worst adversities and emerge truly and beautifully transformed. Like the legendary Phoenix, one can arise from the ashes, more glorious than before.

~ *RaNelle Wallace*

When forged I my greatest strength?

When walked I the longest mile?

When trusted I in faith alone?

'Twas in the hour of trial…

When found I eternal purpose?

When proved I my soul's desire?

When saw I the face of God?

'Twas in the heat of the Refiner's fire.

~LeeAnn Taylor

Stephen Walters

Cindy Cline-Flores

Twenty-four Hours To Live

I was told I had twenty-four hours to live. I remember being wheeled from intensive care to a place I guess you'd call the dying room. This is where they take you when there's really no hope left. I pulled off my oxygen mask while riding on the gurney and asked the nurse, "How long do I have?" At first, she avoided my eyes and acted as if she hadn't heard me. Once again, I asked, and once again, she refused an answer, so I wheezed, "Twenty-four hours?" At this, she cocked her head as if to say "maybe."

One week earlier, a doctor in Taos, New Mexico had told me I had leukemia, and probably had six months to live. Within a couple of days, due to complications, I developed pneumonia. I was on the verge of a heart attack, my white blood cell count was off the charts, and I was suffocating, even while receiving one hundred percent oxygen.

The doctor had prescribed morphine, and I'd basically been tripping for a week. At one point, waking from a drug-induced haze, I looked down at my body and saw right through it to the bed below. My body had become a waving holographic band of floating colors. My brother, noticing the look on my face, asked what was happening. I said, "My body looks like Diana Ross' dress!" Luckily, a dear friend asked if I really wanted to be on morphine. Thank God I was sober enough to understand the question, and shook my head an emphatic "no."

Once the morphine was stopped, I was able to get a better handle on things, and gained the clarity I needed to make my own decisions. I quickly came to realize that morphine and other narcotics are often prescribed more for family, friends, and the hospital staff than for the patient. Nobody wants to see another person suffering, and even if there isn't a lot of physical pain, we all feel better if we think the "dying" person is freed from fear and other emotional pain – even if that means keeping them snowed.

I remember the turning point. The room was filled with friends and family who had come to say goodbye. I realized – true to form – that I was emotionally taking care of everyone in the room but myself. I wanted to say the perfect parting words. I wanted everyone to know that I loved them, and that they were important to me. I wanted the story to have a movie-like perfect ending. I bequeathed my guitar to one friend who replied, "You're not gone yet, Steve," and I left my performance gear to another friend. Then I got it. I realized that if I continued on this way I was going to die. I was losing energy with each passing moment, because I wasn't being with myself! Talk about a life lesson! I whispered to my older brother, Mark, that I needed everyone to leave the room. I sat up in bed, which immediately helped my breathing, and started meditating.

I concentrated deeply on my breathing, remaining very still. I recalled my swim coach in high school asking if I could draw just ten-percent more air into my lungs as I swam. I found maybe one percent, but it was enough. I continued meditating for as long as I could – maybe an hour and a half – and fell asleep. Waking a few hours later, I sat up in bed and started the process again. Each time I fell asleep, I did not know if I would awaken again. This continued for a few more days. Waking, meditating, sleeping. A week later, I was leaving the hospital. One month later, I received a life-saving bone marrow transplant at a hospital in Seattle.

I love sharing this part of the story… Six months prior to being diagnosed, I was in the city of Benares, India with a wonderful spiritual teacher. Many people would come to him for healing and spiritual guidance. I knew that he could "see." I had some premonition of my coming illness and asked him, "Shibu, am I okay?"

He stopped, looked at me with a sweet, yet almost perplexed expression, and simply said, "Everything is perfect." At this point, I knew that I was in fact going to face some major illness, and that everything was, indeed, "perfect."

Here's another quick story I love telling. I remember speaking with Ram Dass on the phone just before the "twenty-four-hour" period. I had been involved with the Neem Karoli Baba Ashram in Taos, New Mexico, and knew a friend who could contact Ram Dass. I can't remember a thing he said, but I recall the strangest thought arising as he spoke. I remember thinking, "Wow! This is pretty cool. I'm dying, and I'm on the phone with Ram Dass!" It's difficult to explain how funny this was. There was the simultaneous awareness of the dire position I was in, yet the absurd thought that I had, at least in a spiritual sense, "made it."

People often ask, after hearing my story, if I survived because I decided to stay. I still don't know the answer to this. At one point, I just realized that the story didn't have to go the way it seemed to be going. I had a willingness to let this life pass, and felt a surprising peace accompanying that willingness. I truly felt okay with whichever way it was going to go. I remember thinking, "Well, that was this life… 38 years." Yet at one point, I just "leaned" a bit more this way… towards life. Once the decision was made to stay, it seemed that all faculties and resources lined up to help support that decision.

Probably the most amazing miracle of all is the sound I am hearing as I write these last words. My five-year-old son Sam is playing with his toys in the back room. Doctors had told me that after all of the chemo, I most likely wouldn't be able to father a child. Well, life obviously has a story of its own to tell.

It is now thirteen years since my transplant. I wish I could say that I live in a state of persistent gratitude, but many of the same challenges I faced before my illness still face me. I am often impatient, short tempered, and self centered. Come to think of it, maybe that's one of the reasons I'm still here.

God's not finished with me yet.

~ *Stephen Walters*

Yvonne Washington, Madison and Vonda Oliver
Photo by Alisa Murray

Cindy Cline-Flores

My Faith
Determined My Outcome

To look at me, you would think I had it all. I was newly wed to my husband, Marvin. I had a loving family and a career I loved. We had just purchased a new home, and I was pregnant with our son. I was living the "American dream." Yet on December 6, 2004, I found myself sitting on my bed, feeling empty as I cried out to God to bring me closer to Him.

My father, Jerrell Washington, had been ill for some time, so I decided to take the day off and help take care of him. While I was in the back of the house, I felt something pop in my body. Suddenly it was if I was on fire, and I couldn't do anything but scream. I called for my dad, who could barely walk himself at the time, and he ran to the phone and called the paramedics.

Although it seemed at that moment that nothing I had planned was going my way, everyone I needed was in place, just as if they had known I was going to go into premature labor. I was only 28 weeks pregnant, and was now in serious danger of losing the baby. As I was rushed to the hospital I was in the worst pain imaginable. All I could do was scream, "Jesus help me!" I had never seen that many nurses and doctors bustling in and out of one room. Then I heard one doctor over all the others: "Everyone will have to wait. I can't hear the baby's heart beat, and the mother is losing too much blood... I'm going to lose them!"

I remember being placed on a gurney, and then people were rushing me to the delivery room. My mother, Yvonne, ran alongside the gurney, and I could see her crying. At that point, I truly began to think the worst.

Our son Madison was born weighing 2lbs., 4oz, and he was nonresponsive. I wasn't doing well at all myself, having lost over 87% of the blood in my body. Doctors informed my husband that neither my son nor I would survive. But by then the waiting room was filled with my loved ones, and they all began to pray. Before long the doctors returned and informed my husband that they could save my son, but to continue to prepare for the worst with regards to my survival. My husband and mother and other loved ones simply continued to pray. Before long I became stable, but now it was clear that the fight for my son's life was just beginning.

The neurologist informed my husband and me that our son had been diagnosed with several brain abnormalities and would never be able to walk or talk. Honestly, our first reaction was grief and confusion. All we could do at that point was continue to pray.

Although my family was there every step of the way, I had never felt so alone, confused, angry, and afraid. After all, this was my baby. I could not believe that this was happening to *my* son. I had always been an advocate for children, had dedicated my life to making their lives better, and now I was being told that my own son wouldn't be able to walk or talk. The next day, I was stricken with an overwhelming sadness. I asked God to bring me closer to Him, and suddenly I found myself crying. Then as I cried, I began to scream. And before I knew it, I was screaming, "Thank you God!" My sister sat beside me in utter disbelief. She could not believe that with all I was going through, I was still thanking God. It was at that point that I truly understood and proclaimed everything my pastor had taught us. I felt that I was finally standing on the firm foundation of the word of God.

I vowed to study His word more, and to fast for a year, thanking God in advance for the miracle that I knew beyond a doubt was going to take place.

Many children in Madison's unit did not survive. I believe that God placed me in one of the most uncompromising and humbling positions possible in order to allow me to minister and pray with the mothers of those babies. They were going through the same thing I was, but worse. I don't know if I was able to make a difference in their lives, but I do know that what happened to Madison has changed my family, making our faith even stronger than before.

Madison did not have an easy time of it in his first days. He was placed on a heart monitor, a respirator (twice), a feeding tube, and oxygen. He received two blood transfusions and was clinically diagnosed with agenesis of the corpus colossum, with additional brain abnormalities. Yet during the entire time he was in the hospital, there were nurses and staff that cared for him as if he were their own son. I honestly believe that they were his "angels on earth."

After three months of being hospitalized, Madison was transferred to the second level, which meant he would be coming home soon. By then he was alert and able to breathe on his own, and could drink out of a bottle. He was still on an apnea monitor, however, and there was still the troubling brain diagnosis. We requested a second MRI.

Cindy Cline-Flores

I remember praying for my son before he received the second MRI. People circled my mother and father as they touched my back and I touched my son. As tears ran down my face, I began to thank God for the miracle in healing my son, and for the difference he would make in this world. People we didn't know joined in the prayer. One woman of Muslim faith even joined in the prayer, proclaiming that Jesus Christ is Lord.

Within 48 hours, the doctor called me in to tell me that the abnormalities from the first MRI were no longer there. I graciously thanked her for the news, but informed her that I knew the answer before I entered the room.

We are now getting ready to celebrate Madison's fifth birthday. He is a very healthy, vibrant, energetic, active, and talkative little boy. I truly believe that if I had begun to feel sorry for myself and give up, our situation would be completely different. I am profoundly grateful for the hospital staff who helped save my son, for the friends and family who surrounded me throughout my time of trouble, and for the God who never let me forget that there is *always hope.*

~ *Vonda Washington*

Lowell Quentin Bass
Photo by Alisa Murray

Cindy Cline-Flores

Overcoming "Woundology": One Man's Story

The second "war to end all wars," the largest war ever fought, had finally come to an end. Hitler's reign had ended, and other dictators' malicious agendas in Europe and the Pacific Rim had proven unsuccessful. Tens of thousands of weary young service men and women in Europe and on other military bases across the globe could finally go home! But the war had taken a huge toll on the psyche of our nation and the entire global community. The cost in both treasure and blood was monumental, beyond anything that had come before or since. The A-bomb had been dropped, the horrific Holocaust was over, and it was at long last time for nation-building and deep global soul-searching, and for our wounded planet to begin healing and putting lives back together again. This new post-war effort was our fresh start, the beginning of an unprecedented expansion period for America and the world. It was a new era of hope.

At the time the United States was plunged into the Second World War, the country had barely made it out of the Great Depression. Sometimes it is difficult for me to believe I was born a mere decade after the final crushing blows of that catastrophic time in history. At the time of my birth, the country was still reeling under the bitter physical, financial, and emotional toll of the past couple of decades. There was no escaping the deep and troubling scars the Depression had left behind, and with the war having just ended, it was as if the very air were tainted with the toils, blood, and anguish that the greater world had endured. Nevertheless, the country seemed intent upon relishing its post-war jubilation. This triumphant spirit wasn't confined to America; people throughout the world who loved freedom reveled in their enormous victories. It was a time for mass celebrations, a time to move forward, and a time for humankind to evolve beyond the horrors of its recent past.

For some, however, this new American Dream remained painfully elusive.

My dad was one of the hundreds of thousands of courageous American military people returning home at long last. Like so many, he had fought a good fight, but now it was time for him to once again be with his family, to rejoin his high school sweetheart, get married, and begin a family in southeast Michigan. He was beside himself, for his big dreams and his plans for a joyous future could finally come true.

The first step he took towards realizing his dreams was to marry my mother shortly after his return. Not long after they got married, I was born, the second of seven children. My first home was in a public housing project near Detroit, which everyone in the inner city simply referred to as "The Projects." As was the case with so many Negroes of that time – it would be many years before we would be known as African-Americans! – our economic condition and social status were dramatically different than they are today. They were certainly different from those living with the advantage of privilege and power.

Unfortunately, the huge "post-war expansion" was not universal, and the successes experienced by some failed to trickle down to everyone. A large segment of Americans were left out. Far too many felt that their promise, their dreams, and their hopes fell futile. Many people who shared the same hopes and dreams were left stranded on the outside, looking in at others who were living the dreams that they had themselves been denied. Among those on the sidelines were my neighbors, my playmates, and my relatives. And many of them shared the same historical background, having been brought as slaves into a country supposedly founded upon freedom. During my formative years, there were two different Americas: one of inclusion and empowerment, the other of segregation and oppression. Blighted but ignored neighborhoods were plentiful. Injustice was blatant, and there was no public cry for change. Many in positions of power just looked away, and those who could make things better didn't. Any demands were met with either a deaf ear or swift reprimands and rejection – especially within our legal system.

Mass social reforms, civil-rights legislation, and major equal rights were still a couple of decades away. The idealistic young Kennedy men, President Johnson with his visions of the Great Society, and Dr. Martin Luther King, Jr. with his famous dream for a truly united America, would all do their part one day to usher in a new era of humanitarianism and equality. Because of these men's efforts and those of countless other men and women, there would come a time when a person's skin color, gender, social class, or nationality would no longer automatically eliminate him or her from full participation in American life. It would no longer be legal, and would no longer be accepted as moral, to deny whole groups of legal citizens their right to inclusion in housing, schools, jobs, and religious institutions. It would no longer be acceptable for people to

Cindy Cline-Flores

routinely label, objectify, and then step over others in the march to realize their own dreams. Only then would the very fabric of our culture shift for the better, and only then could many of the past wounds begin to heal.

But all of that was still in the future. The 1940s and 1950s were the Truman and Eisenhower years, and unfortunately, none of us had a crystal ball that allowed us to see what the future would hold. The mere hope of change seemed centuries away. Even safe havens like the church and family couldn't shield those on the "outside" from the many problems plaguing our great land. Those who were unable to hang in there, to be patient, to get busy and ride it out lost hope. Bitter resignation and cynicism filled the void where dreams once had dwelt, and distrust and despair were easy to find. On one side of most cities and towns, there were soda fountains with jukeboxes playing swing tunes and be-bop, while mere blocks away, in the areas where kids like me grew up, there were honky-tonks and dope houses, where a people lacking hope could at least numb themselves. Hundreds of thousands of people fell prey to easier vices, giving in to their darkest sides of themselves just to escape. But even in those places, and even when our eyes don't see it, there is always hope!

It didn't take a Ph.D. from an Ivy League school, the action of our nation's Supreme Court, or boycotts and marches for me to recognize that things were far from right. Even at the age of four, it was clear to me that I too was being labeled and boxed into a parallel world over which I had little say, much less control. The incongruity of those parallel worlds was evident in my everyday life, and was only reinforced by the explicit and constant reminders on national television, newspapers, and magazines. These media constantly discussed matters such as health, wealth, higher education, and leisure in a way that made the glaring reality of this gigantic divide painfully clear. Locally, all it took for children like me to see the sharp contrast between "their" world and our own was a trip downtown, or to the beautifully manicured city parks, or a field trip to the one of the many ivy-covered buildings on the university campus. That "other" America was so alien to me that I could have just as well been living on the moon. I was an outsider in my own country.

In the early '50s we left the housing project and moved into a beat-up house less than six blocks away from the city's toxic dump. The condition of that house was worse than the projects. The words my sister and I used to describe it were "sad and ugly." It looked like a dump itself, but felt more like a dungeon. Indeed, something was off – really, really off!

This house was only a hundred feet or so from Skid Row, the place where African-American social, business, and residential life converged. The area was full of sultry, funky bars, scandalous pool halls, crowded barbershops, loud beauty salons, lip-smacking soul food restaurants, cramped and dirty liquor stores, and small but busy neighborhood grocery stores.

My senses were constantly bombarded with the sounds of heavy blues and razor-sharp jazz music, along with the loud noise of car horns honking, doors slamming, and the fussing, fighting, and cursing of patrons floating into my open bedroom window. On weekend nights and well into the wee hours of morning, it was like being in one huge honky-tonk echo chamber. Even the occasional gunshot rang out into the night air. The air was always laden with the smells of cigar and cigarette smoke, whiskey, beer, ribs, fried chicken and fish, greens, burgers, and fries. It was an endless parade of different people going various places, many for reasons that were obvious. You name it; it was there. Businessmen and businesswomen, locals and out-of-towners, druggies, winos, prostitutes, hustlers, clergy, church folk, workers, fruit vendors, seniors, children, and more, all swirled up together and converged into a never-ending community rhythm.

My own life seemed off-kilter from the time when I was barely out of diapers. It's hard to explain, but I always had the strong feeling of not really fitting in with my chaotic and troubled environment. My dreams, my view of the world around me, and even the way I viewed my core self were clearly very different from so many others around me. I was hopeful and passionate, brimming over with the sense of possibility, with big dreams and bigger plans. While others seemed to just go along and fit in, I never could and never did. Even in my own neighborhood, I simply could not stay in "my place." I didn't know how to fake it, and wouldn't have tried even if I had known how. It perplexed me how people would just go along with life and not take an in-depth look at themselves. I couldn't be like that. But who could I share my insights with? Who would understand? Who would even bother to hear me? When I tried to articulate these questions, I was told just to suck it up.

Like so many other kids in the inner-city and poorer neighborhoods across America, I lived my life continually on a thin ledge and on high alert. Concerns for our basic safety and security were always there, right on the surface. Life was raw, even for children. Our elementary school was located on the main drag, just a block or two away from the strip where so many grown-ups went to escape their frustrations. School life for us was nothing at all like the simplistic stories we read in our primers of Dick, Jane, Sally, and their pets Spot the dog and Puff the cat. It was more like a wild urban-thriller variation of *The Color Purple*, where life was in constant flux, a spiral of losses and struggles. Dick and Jane's real-life counterparts were a world away from us, for busing was not an option in those days. During our early grade school years, what our young eyes, ears, and souls were exposed to provided an education in itself. From kindergarten onward, my peers and I became quite skillful, streetwise in navigating to and from school each day, through and beyond all of the confusion, temptations, and chaos in the streets.

It was a skill that paid off for me many times later in life.

In our own household, the attitude was that as long as the basics were taken care of – as long as we were warm, dry, and fed – there was nothing to complain about, nothing whatsoever to be concerned about. What was the big deal? Yet in actuality, there were many intense and deeply troubling issues at play, lurking right beneath the surface, impacting not only me but my two siblings who were closest to my own age. For us, our home was no safe haven.

The home environment in those early years was often erratic and unpredictable, and that is putting it mildly. It was like living inside of a ticking time-bomb, subject to go off at any time, for any reason. It's often said that parenting doesn't come with an instruction manual, that parenting is not an exact art. My young parents were certainly an illustration of this truism. They got better at parenting as time went by, but in the early years, just about every mistake a parent could make seemed to be played out in our lives, in a seemingly endless vicious cycle.

My dad was a tall, fit, and very charming man with large dreams and even larger visions. He was a sharp dresser who made a great impression in every social situation. Well-liked and pleasant to talk to, he possessed an impressive knowledge of a great many subjects. Dad's military background and experience in Europe had only enhanced his knowledge base, and he was well aware of that. Unfortunately, what my father had envisioned for himself and his family was a whole lot different from what he got. The ends just never seemed to match up. His big picture and big vision never seemed to come into focus, and the family reality that played out was skewed and almost always out of balance. This would frustrate him to no end, eating at him a lot in his younger years and my own formative years.

Unfortunately, when push came to shove, all of Dad's gifts and talents often didn't count in those days; they just weren't enough. As you can imagine, those were still not the easiest of times for a black man, with or without children, to find and keep steady work. It was an enormous challenge for Dad to simply keep a roof over our heads and food in our stomachs, to say nothing of having any extra left over to do some planning that would move his family ahead just a bit more. For Dad it was always about progress, about moving us forward. Despite the numerous setbacks, he was driven to succeed. And he was a proud man, refusing to accept food stamps and assistance because he saw those things as a trap. Yet he couldn't seem to get ahead on his own, and had to make new starts over and over again. After a few too many times, the process took its toll.

One way of dealing with his frustrations was to drink, and that would make him angrier about his situation, which led to more drinking, and then more anger, and more drinking… you get the idea. This happened over and over. Where were all of the "good times" we were always hearing about? Where was the promise? "The good times" rarely showed themselves to us; we only got brief and vague glimpses from time to time. As for the promise, the outside world seemed to hold little enough of that, and at home, Dad set the mood, which all too often was dark and defensive. He would transform from an approachable, open man to an intolerant and narrow man far too many times. I understand now what I didn't always understand then: whenever he encountered disappointment and despair in the streets, there would be "hell to pay" at home.

As far as I know my dad was never physically violent with Mom, but he was much too often violent with us kids, particularly me and my younger brother who was closest to me in age. It was tough to sit on pins and needles most of the time. We would be petrified, often keeping quiet so as not to provoke the slightest reaction. Lord knows we didn't want him upset! More often than not, however, it was out of our control. When he would come home, especially with the whiff of strong raw liquor on his breath, it usually meant that anything would go. There was extreme physical, verbal, psychological, and even spiritual abuse, with a few other types added on. These fiery rampages were generally followed by many regrets, which he didn't express directly to us.

My mom had her own issues, her own painful baggage. Her mother had been murdered when she was still a small girl in the 1920s, and that terrible event cast long dark sad shadows into her life. It was a loss from which she never completely recovered, and it bled over into most aspects of her teenage and adult life. I have no doubt that it affected her own mothering skills. Like my father, she was physically, psychologically, and verbally abusive to us children. Her lengthy bouts of depression and episodes of emotional withdrawal were too numerous to count. It seemed that she was always "zigging" and "zagging" back and forth, with little consistency. We all felt her pain, and it caused us pain as well. She was physically right there in front of us, but emotionally unavailable.

In short, there was a lot of drama in my home when I was growing up. "Moderation" was a concept that seemed alien to both of our parents in the earlier years, and we kids paid the price.

In school, I had another set of problems, but it was here that I would also get my first big breakthrough. I had reading challenges, and found it extremely difficult to communicate what I was thinking and feeling. The skills which I had such difficulty acquiring are a core part of learning and expressing oneself, and I recall being immensely frustrated with both of these shortcomings. However, when I would try to express my frustration to others, their typical response was to dismiss or trivialize my feelings. This troubled me greatly. I was at least several grades behind my peers in my reading ability, yet I excelled in classes where those skills were not involved. Still, I fell further behind in areas where communicating and reading were essential.

Cindy Cline-Flores

Who could hear my concerns and feel my aggravation? Nobody, it seemed; I found not one compassionate ear. I felt alone, embarrassed, disempowered. The impatience I encountered from people who couldn't figure out why I could not get what seemed to come so natural to others was exceeded by my impatience with myself. This seeming paradox amazed and bewildered me at the same time. The answer seemed beyond me, beyond my knowing.

In spite of my limitations I never failed a grade (unlike my younger brother, who had his own emotional challenges). I passed from first grade to second, and from second to third, and from third to fourth. I began the fourth grade with mixed feelings, looking forward to advancing my education, yet still haunted by my difficulties with speaking and reading. I was never at peace with my limitations, so it was with some trepidation that I entered my fourth grade classroom for the first time.

There I beheld a lovely young woman who was open, warm, and smiling. When she opened her mouth and spoke, I was knocked off my feet. She had a very thick accent of a kind that I did not recognize but found very cool. I had never been that close up to anyone who spoke in that particular way, with those types of voice inflections. I was certainly familiar with the Southern drawl, because many people had moved from an economically depressed South to Michigan to gain employment at one of the "Big Three" automobile companies. The Southern migration during that time was massive, and a good percentage of my schoolmates and their parents spoke with that accent. But my new teacher's dialect was neither Southern nor Northeastern. No, hers was different, and utterly enchanting to me.

Her name was Joan Bing. She was from Great Britain, and a recent graduate of the University of Michigan. Miss Bing and I connected instantly. She saw and related to me in a different way than any of my other teachers or anyone else in my life had done. In the 1950s in the inner city, a teacher from a different land – a different world – was almost unheard of. Indeed, she brought a broad range of new perceptions and skills into our classroom. To me, her presence in my life was an outright miracle. She could connect deep inside my soul, look into me, and see me in a new and powerful way that no one else had ever been able to do. I felt understood for the very first time in my life, and that bond called out, demanding the very best from me. I loved it. I thrived.

My walls came down and as trust showed up, I became open and transparent. I was already ripe and ready to improve, more than ready to overcome the burden of my two big liabilities. All I needed was the right teacher. There's an old saying to the effect that when the student is ready, the teacher will show up. And I can't think of a better illustration of the truth of this saying than the example of myself and my fourth-grade teacher. Because of her compassion, patience, acceptance, and uncanny knowledge, I began to apply myself in a different and more complete way. I excelled in areas I was unable to excel in earlier. Before long my reading and even my overall learning skills improved dramatically.

This was the very first time in my young life that I ever made a deep connection with an adult, and I was grateful and deeply honored by our connection. To this day I believe that she was an angel sent to me just at the right time. My resistance to learning subsided, and for that entire school year she taught me, privately mentored me, and opened me up to new models of learning, and whole new worlds. She created an unconditional "zone" where it was perfectly okay for me to not know anything – just to be in a state of inquiry about everything. I had prayed for this, without even knowing precisely what I was praying for. It now seemed clear that she embodied all I had asked for. It was she who aided me in starting a new chapter in my life around the mastery of words, language, and education. Where there had been no answer in sight, there now came a rushing cascade of insights. Where there had been frustration, there now came a sense of fulfillment and adventure. For the first time I felt a balance in my body, my mind, and my soul. I felt a quality of self-dignity and self-respect I had never known. I began to build upon that, never forgetting the beautiful gifts that were given to me.

This teacher was the first to introduce me to the beauty and the love of learning. There would be many, many others over the years who shared the same love, passion, and commitment to education, and who helped me truly understand the joy of learning and creating. What a powerful, priceless, and life-changing gift this was, and Miss Bing was the one who first offered it to me. From that point, my life took on a new trajectory, full of passion and hope. I was finally on a path, and no longer stuck in a pit.

I must say, however, that reading was easier to tackle than my speaking abilities. I had great difficulty clearly formulating my words and ideas, especially if I did not know or trust someone. It wasn't that I was shy or withdrawn, not at all. The issue was that when I would try to formulate my thoughts, my beliefs and passion and feelings were all so strong that I had difficulty singling out words and stringing them together in coherent ways. I was crystal clear in my soul about the feeling I intended to convey, but putting the strings of words together and pushing them out from my body was something altogether different. It was a huge problem for me, and the harder I tried, the faster I would ramble. It was only later that I was able to overcome this challenge.

It would have been wonderful if everyone in my young life had been as understanding and open-minded as Miss Bing, but this was far from the case. All too often I was limited by the restrictions placed on me by the adults in my life. I was frustrated by their constant efforts to edit me, to censor me, and often to stop me from moving forward with my ideas, my thoughts, and even my dreams. It sometimes seemed that the entire world was out to disempower me, to render me as the invisible little boy. But I fought back, over and over again… I was not going out like that! I was always hopeful, my big dream being that one day the feelings inside me would match the words I spoke out into the world. I knew me very well, knew the potential inside of me, and it seemed a huge contradiction that the world around me was not similarly aware. Most frustrating of all was the fact that even in my own home I often felt as if I was not known. This only reinforced my challenges with self-expression, which in turn seemed to make the "censors" in my life more determined in their mission to silence me… and there I was, caught up in another vicious cycle.

As I said above, all of this changed over time. It would take me another decade or so to overcome my issues around speech and speaking. It was not until my early twenties that I became fully competent with my speech. But I never stopped practicing and applying, practicing and applying, and then practicing some more, again and again. I learned how to learn. I never stopped trying. My hope never waned.

In my adult life I had many more challenges to overcome, including alcohol and food addictions, the isolation that comes from being an overachiever, and temporary estrangement from my family. I could have ended up making a real mess of my life. The one thing that kept me from doing so was that I never, ever gave up hope.

You may wonder what became of my parents. The story of their earlier years together reads like the setup for a tragic ending, and it very well could have been. But our family was blessed. Many of the deep-rooted personal issues both of my parents faced as young adults and young parents were tempered by time. By then I had grown up, moved out, and moved on to college and beyond. Slowly but surely, my parents' lives – not to mention their parenting – began to improve. I can see now that in some ways they were well-intentioned, especially as I reached my early teen years, but they both lacked the emotional nurturing skills desired and often required by young teens. We older children didn't get the direct benefit of my folks' shift in maturity, but our younger siblings certainly did. They were better cared for, and I am deeply grateful for that.

I should also note that despite their personal demons, my parents were valued and deeply respected by many people in our community. As time went by, they became an inspiration wherever they would go. My dad never stopped trying and reaching for his own golden treasure at the end of the rainbow, and I am glad to report that it did come before he passed. In time, he achieved the financial success he had hoped for. He also became a remarkable grandfather with many grandchildren, and a mentor to many people of all ages in his church and elsewhere. He always had hope, even in the shakiest of times. He never, ever stopped dreaming and reaching for his dream. My dad was a remarkable man, and I say that as one who bore the brunt of a disproportionate share of his earlier acting out. People can and do change. Hope does count, and it is very important to keep it alive.

Mom and Dad remained in love and together for the entire fifty-plus years of their marriage, until their recent deaths. Despite their troubled lives in their earlier years, they found much greater peace and fulfillment as they grew older. Both Mom and Dad apologized many times to my siblings and me. They made their amends to us. For my part, I loved them both and forgave them both. And I have found that forgiveness – whether you are on the giving or the receiving end – is a gift as powerful and sweet as hope.

Another great gift I have gained from my life experience is the knowledge that I – and all of us – have the power of choice along every phase of our journey in life, and we must each walk our own walk. But I cannot overstate the importance of forgiveness and love. When we are able to see and love each other in spite of our blemishes and flaws, our own personal journey becomes all the more valuable and joyful. We can warehouse our resentments, we can continue to keep score of all the misdeeds of others and everything that didn't work out, we can persist in our efforts to prove ourselves right and others wrong. Or we can simply trust ourselves enough to know that we are all human and subject to making mistakes.

The biggest gift we can give ourselves lies not in "proving ourselves right." Rather, it lies in getting ourselves – and our lives – over those hurdles of "woundology," so we can embrace our own healing and allow others the space to heal as well. Don't be greedy or stingy with your journey. Paradoxically, you can learn to be generous and share yourself only if you truly step out of yourself and beyond your pain. When you move beyond your "woundology" you are better able to share yourself more fully with your own self, your family, your friends, your city, your nation, the world… the entire human race. It's your choice! Even when you can't see it, hope is always there.

I faced tremendous disadvantages when I was growing up. Living near a toxic city dump as a child was a poignant metaphor for what my life so easily could have been; many thought that I too would end up in a scrap heap. Instead, I look upon my life as a journey from grit to glory, a reflection of serendipity at work. But my life is also a reflection of choices I made along the way; serendipity can only do so much, after all!

Each of us needs to remember that this is our life, and we get to choose. When we heal and free ourselves – with straight talk, and without skirting the issues, but with unconditional love – we unconsciously become an example for others. As we free ourselves, we help others to free themselves. When we let our unconditional love light shine, we unconsciously give other people the license, the freedom, the permission to do the same. There is great liberating power in this. I value the wisdom in the children's church song: "This little light of mine, I'm gonna let it shine… let it shine, let it shine, let it shine!"

My wish for you is that you will let your light shine too, and that no matter what happens, you never lose sight of the fact that there is *Always Hope.*

~ *Lowell Quentin Bass*

Christina Webb
Photo by Alisa Murray

Cindy Cline-Flores

The Power Within: Becoming Who We Are

My story is a story about becoming who we really are. It's about breaking the shackles that bind and limit us. These are not physical shackles, although there are some people in this world who have been bound in that way also. The most insidious shackles are those that have been formed in our minds by the world around us when we were little children. Yet this is not a story about blame, because blame is merely another shackle that dwells in our psyche, taking up space where other more beautiful thoughts and feelings could reside. A powerful truth is to know is that we have the key to our freedom. It can be hard turning the key to get to that freedom, but the perseverance in trying is not only worthwhile, but essential, and the satisfaction of ultimately succeeding is the most fantastic feeling in the world.

I won't go into all of the details of my past here, because it is the lessons, not the details, that are important. Suffice it to say that, like so many others, I grew up in an atmosphere of extreme negativity. Different circumstances perhaps, but the message is the same: "You're no good." "You're too fat." "Stupid!" "You better be perfect." "Can't you do anything right?" And on and on…. you get the picture. I heard many of these as I was growing up.

And then there was the physical abuse. Today, I can see that it was caused by the frustration of my parents' longing for self-fulfillment, and by the unresolved, unhealed hurt and pain that they passed down to their children – my two siblings and me. It was the type of rage that, if ignored, has nowhere to go except to be passed down from generation to generation. The legacy of this rage is a child with a stifled ability to believe in his or her greatness. I was one of those children.

But the beautiful thing, the most awesome realization from having this life experience, is to find an incredible power and Presence, sometimes hidden deep inside. Perhaps it is more accurate to say that it finds us, speaks to us, and wakes us up – that is, if we are listening carefully. And it comes forth to show us the way to break the shackles and live victoriously.

I think that some of us are much more sensitive than others to the effects the world has on us. I now know that I am a highly sensitive person (there is a book written about this 15-20% population, *The Highly Sensitive Person*, by Elaine N. Aron, Ph.D.). I believe this is why the effects that my upbringing had on me lasted well into my forties, only dissipating after I did deep healing work. Of course I have heard it said, "Yeah, everybody's got something from their childhood; just move on and get on with life…. stop whining." But it simply is not that easy for some.

I look at who I have become, and I marvel at the journey. My sojourn of recovery began when I found my spiritual home at Unity Church in Houston. When I began that journey, I did not know who I was. I had been conditioned for my focus in life to be on others, to be a caretaker. I had no sense of what I needed to do in order to take care of myself. My self-esteem was so shaky that I could not speak in front of more than two people without retreating into the abyss of self-loathing. My words, as far as I was concerned, were worthless. I felt I didn't have anything worthwhile to say. My self-judgments were harsh to the point of being debilitating; I was unable to communicate authentically and comfortably. It was so painful to be hiding the real me, but the fear that others around me would not like me, the real me, smothered my ability to be – much less express – who I was. Only with my closest friends could I let down my guard and be myself.

This also carried over to an inability to think that I could achieve anything worthwhile or that I could do exciting things in life like "those other" people who enjoyed life, who accomplished things, who were successful. So I went through the dramas of my life – abuse of drugs and alcohol, failed marriages, single parenthood at near-poverty level – and I weathered the storms that accompanied these experiences.

It was at Unity that my life turned around. I think everyone recognizes the feeling of "coming home." Well, to me, Unity was my new home. As I started to face my demons and uncover the roots that bound me to the past, I began to take the messages I heard at Unity, messages that resonated deep within me as the absolute Truth and gradually changed my thoughts. As I changed my thoughts – and for many of us it is a gradual experience because of the patterns being so deeply rooted – my life started to change in miraculous ways.

I came to realize that I had actually been blessed, even in the midst of these challenges, in many wonderful aspects of my life. Even though my car was an oldie, it took me where I needed to go. Yes, I was raising three children on a waitress wage, but hey, the bills were paid and we had food to eat. I may not have had a high-end home, but it was comfortable and in a nice neighborhood with good schools. My children and I were all extremely healthy, and in spite of our woes, we made the best of it and had a lot of love. And to top it all off, I had found a beautiful place to be around like-minded people and to celebrate my spirituality. As I realized my blessings, I became aware of the serene gratitude I felt, instead of griping about what I didn't have. And because of the law of attraction, as I kept my focus on the positives in my life, my prosperity increased in all areas: not just in finances, but also in relationships, health, and spirituality.

Along with the increased awareness of life's beauty and the blessings my family and I enjoyed came the awesome unfolding of my real self, my Christ self, which, through continued meditation, prayer, self-examination, and healing, blossomed and grew. I began to feel better and better about myself, in my realization that it was only I who didn't accept myself the way I truly was. My loving, unconditionally accepting creator didn't judge me, and loved me just as I was. It was I who needed to forgive, accept and release the judgments about myself that limited me. As I peeled away the layers of doubt, self-loathing, and shame, I stepped out of my comfort zone, stretching and growing in ways I never, ever would have imagined in my earlier years.

I believe we all have something to fulfill in our lives. It may be a big purpose that takes us into world prominence. Or it may be healing or lessons to be learned that have brought us to this lifetime. Or it could be anything in between. If we open ourselves up to Spirit, continually ask and are self aware, we can know what it is. We may never know on a conscious level. But our soul knows.

I feel I have come into this world, with the trials and tribulations along the way, to share, by the written word or by speaking to others, the insights and lessons I have learned in overcoming hardship. Surely, there have been others who have been through more than I. But that's not the point. It's not a contest. We all can contribute to the encouragement and uplifting of mankind. That is what feeds my soul.

So, in a nutshell, I did break the shackles that bound my mind and limited my potential. Spirit said, "I want you to go out and tell the world." I followed that voice and studied, over a ten-year period, to become a Licensed Unity Teacher, which gave me the opportunity to get up in front of others and help facilitate their spiritual unfoldment. I was also able to serve as a speaker at different spiritual venues. And to top it off, as I came to the realization and acceptance of my true self, I experienced the ultimate freedom of being able to express myself in a spectrum of authentic ways, one of which was unbridled joy and the ability to laugh at myself and see the light side of life. At that point, I discovered a way to teach joy to the world, to help others remember the healing power of being joyful and expressing it through laughter. The ultimate expression of authenticity and glee came in becoming a Certified Laughter Leader through *The World Laughter Tour.* I came to realize what Spirit had in store for me as I made my way around the Houston area, speaking to groups as small as five and as large as four hundred, modeling for them hilarious laughter exercises as they followed, participated in, and experienced the true joy within themselves as well.

My fear of speaking and expressing my true self had been conquered through the power of aligning myself with the God within; the God of true, unconditional acceptance, power, peace and joy. And if I could do it, so can you!

~ Christina Webb

Always Hope

Madeline Westbrook
Photo by Alisa Murray

Cindy Cline-Flores

The Ghostwriter And The Muse

I was born with a song in my heart and a book in my hand. I glided through childhood, singing and reading. My family saw me as a happy, mystical child. My daddy nicknamed me "Pollyanna" because I reminded him of the fictional character that constantly looked for good.

When I was fifty-nine, I'd been married for forty one years, had three sons, three daughters-in-law, and four grandchildren. Still like Pollyanna, I always looked for the best. Then...

Parents never plan for things like those that happened to us on New Year's Eve 1994. One week after my sixtieth birthday, our middle son Josh died. His good looks – his blue eyes, bright with intelligence and hope for the future – were gone; his earthly songs silenced, his books unfinished. He was not yet forty years old. The doctors said he died of an unusual type of brain cancer. It doesn't matter what the age or how your child dies, the hurt is the same. Conversely, nothing else in your life is ever the same again. There is no such thing as a time when parents want to accept the death of their child. Some never accept it.

Our son was a lawyer. He was also a writer who dreamed of a full-time writing career. He set things in motion for his new career when he signed up for a novel writing class taught by a well-known professor at a large university in Texas. Our son and I had long discussions about his writing and the inspiration that comes to us through music. When he became ill, he planned to develop his talent and advance it along with a miraculous medical recovery that he believed would come. He would write about overcoming disasters in life.

Though he was more than optimistic, we still talked about dying as he went through the rigors of treatment for his brain cancer. Faced with the basic thoughts on living and dying, we began a dialog that strangely and hauntingly continues to this day.

"Mom, if I should die before you, let's make a plan to forever stay connected. You can tell the family about it someday. You could write about it. What kind of life would we be living if death cuts us away from our loved ones? Let's think about the angel possibilities. With God's help, we could plan this out; call it an experiment, the engineering feat of all time. Build a bridge from the edge of eternity. What do you think?"

People often make deathbed plans and promises. No matter how unrealistic, no matter how irrational, inventive and Divine Ideas are soothing to breaking hearts and troubled minds.

I said, "Of course, I will help build the bridge." In reality, I felt I was dying. I walked outside to the hospital chapel and fell on my knees to plead with God.

When I returned, our son said, "We could do it this way, Mom. We could plan to send musical and written messages. That is, I could send you the messages. You could ask me to send the messages and we could arrange times to connect. If there are special times when we need one another, we could use special signals."

He continued, "You could write my books, you could write our books. My mom, the ghostwriter! I will be your heavenly muse. We could use your favorite radio stations – or anywhere you hear music – for musical messages. You will know. Moreover, when there is an especially important time, there will be something undeniable, something you could prove to the world. At times, we could call on bagpipes." Being of Scottish/Irish descent, this notion certainly resonated with me.

Then, near the end, we made this promise to each other: We would write his books. We would find our inspiration in words written and music heard. There would be serendipitous feelings in writing and mystical messages heard through music. Bagpipes would have special meanings. Words and music would guide each step in our after-death adventure. We would always be a part of each other through our spirits. He and I would set an example for the family, and especially his young children, so as they grew they would know he would be there for them in their own quests of writing and love of music. There would be signs in nature. His spirit would be with us, one way or another.

Shortly after our son died, I bought a computer, a software program for students (grades 5-12), and signed up for the novel writing classes taught by our son's professor at the university. I didn't know anything about the computer. I didn't have an advanced education. I bluffed my way through. I knew I would learn and be guided.

At the end of each semester, the professor required his students to prepare a folder containing our completed assignments and a written narrative in which we made "application to proceed" to the next level of the course. We had to convince the professor we had a reason to continue. If all the assignments were complete and we passed the test in our application to proceed, we would be admitted to the next level of the class. As the levels advanced, the number of students declined. The professor was a demanding teacher.

Soon, I found myself on an almost unbelievable adventure. I had a promise to keep. As I wrote our story, wonders happened. My son's dreams became my dreams. I wrote, taking notes while listening to the radio. I wrote while attending the symphony. I wrote as words and music seemed to come from within a huge "circle of life" surrounding me.

In my writing class, I progressed through levels one, two, three, four, and five. Finally, in late 1997, I was admitted to the advanced level of novel writing. My world had changed. Now, I was living with a book in my heart and music in the air. My mentor, teacher, and guide was a brilliant man born in India, a mystical muse strangely connected to our son's spirit. Though bouts of sadness frequently overtook me, I was compelled to keep the promise we had made.

I was in the midst of writing our novel, our story of love and life that reaches beyond death, when our beloved professor, who was in his fifties, cautiously, carefully, and tenderly announced he had been diagnosed with cancer. In all too familiar courageous tones, the professor began to make his own plans to overcome and recover from his illness. He asked for and received permission from the hospital to continue classes with a few students. He invited the members of the advanced class to gather outside the wall of his isolation cubicle at the nearby cancer hospital. The professor said, "We will continue our assignments and readings. We will gather in small groups at different times of the day and continue our important works." He prepared us by saying, "I will be living behind glass walls for as long as it takes. We will continue our classes until we complete our work." The key word was always "continue."

Memories of our son and his cancer treatments overwhelmed me. I wanted to break and run. I shook with fear as I entered the same doors at the same hospital our son once entered.

The professor critiqued us, peering from behind glass walls, and spoke to us over a telephone as we studied his face and body movements for hopeful signs of improvement. Sadly, none came. Eventually, the classes ceased, but I continued my personal visits with the professor. As the end neared and I spoke with my friend and mentor, I shared with him my reasons for taking his class and our son's plans to stay connected through his classroom. Written words. Music. The professor encouraged me to write the story of love beyond death. He talked about our son and the loss he felt when he died. On one of our last visits, the professor said to me in his finely tuned, British-influenced East Indian accent, "You know, I was looking for your son when you came into class and I found you." He sighed deeply, his dark eyes brimmed with tears. "I had no idea you were his mother."

I replied, "Professor, I was looking and listening for our son, and I found you."

"Yes," said the professor, "what a blessing we gave to each other."

As I listened, I realized it could be his last lecture.

On May 3, 1998, a little more than three years after our son died, our beloved teacher, my mentor, our professor, died. I was stunned. Stunned into silence. The music was stilled. Words disappeared.

I tried to work alone on my novel. I tried to find another class. I tried meeting with my classmates when they regularly met without the professor. Nothing worked. I was ready to quit. I was down-spirited and lonely.

Then one day, following a strong urge to visit the cemetery, I sat beside our son's grave and asked for a sign to show me that I could continue. I thought I was imagining the sounds of a bagpipe in the distance. After searching the graveyard, still unable to find the source of the strange and unbelievable sounds – and to prove to myself that I was still sane – I called the cemetery office on my cell phone, and was told that once a year, a man dressed in kilts came to play his bagpipe beside his loved one's resting place.

I slowly drove my car around the cemetery until I found the man dressed in kilts. I got out of the car, found a bench, and listened to the music. As I sat enraptured, the man looked at me and moved my way as he played a tune we had listened to in the hospital, a family favorite, "Danny Boy." Then, as the piper walked away, he played "Auld Lang Syne," the traditional song of New Year's Eve, the date of our son's death.

For myself, for my son, and for the professor, I drew upon my Inner Source and decided to write another application to proceed. As I listened to the music and thought of writing again, a rekindled spark caught with remembrances of my son and our teacher. The love they had firmly and eternally implanted in my heart began to light the way back to our promise. Words and music were near.

My hunch is that there are many "applications to proceed." One step at a time, one word at a time, the book unfolds and the music rustles in the wind.

Consider life and death as applications to proceed. The words and music inside each of us are there to move us forward as we make application to proceed. Consider writing the first sentence, the next chapter, and the next book.

Cindy Cline-Flores

I am in my seventy-fifth year, and there are promises we must keep.

ADDENDUM

Unlikely bagpipers continue to appear to the family in unusual and secluded spots. Signs in nature and mentors in writing have continued to share in the bridge-building experiment.

Stories of these incidents and others are included in my novel, inspired and based on my story, titled *The Ghost Writer and the Muse – Building a Bridge from Eternity.*

Whenever possible, the family stops to interview and take photographs of the pipers we encounter.

~ Madeline Maxine Westbrook

Madeline Westbrook
Photo by Alisa Murray

Alisa Murray

Cindy Cline-Flores

Alisa Murray:
A Portrait Of The Artist

Everyone has heard the saying, "A picture is worth a thousand words." Rocker Rod Stewart had a hit song some years back called, "Every Picture Tells A Story." You have only to look at the work of Alisa Murray, whose photographs grace the pages of this book, to see the truth in the old maxim and the song title. As one of the most sought-after professional photographers in the United States, Alisa uses her camera to tell some of the most poignant and beautiful stories imaginable. She clearly takes pride in her work, understanding the power of an artist to make a difference in people's lives. Above all, she is profoundly aware of the significance of portraits and their unique ability to immortalize their subjects.

Not unlike the many people featured in *Always Hope*, Alisa has lived through dramatic stories of her own, and these have helped mold her as a person and an artist. When she was only eight years old her mother died – a tragedy in and of itself, but one that had lasting effects on Alisa's development. Though Alisa's mother was only thirty-one when she passed away, she had made quite an impact in her community in her brief lifetime. She implemented a program that brought focus to violence on TV and the negative influences that media have on children. In addition, she created a special reading program for gifted students to learn the classics such as *Moby Dick*. In the year of her death, she was nominated for "Woman of the Year."

It seemed that in the wake of her mother's death, the adults in Alisa's life were incapable of moving on. The problem was exacerbated because Alisa looked just like her deceased mother, which made it very hard for the young girl to define who she was, and more difficult still to fully understand the adults around her. "Many times I was asked to wear my mom's clothes, and as I grew into a young woman my family would 'accidentally' call me by her name," Alisa says. "When I went to church, some of the members of the choir would start crying at the very sight of me. And one close friend used to say that to look at me was to stare at my mother's ghost."

As you can imagine, Alisa's childhood was a difficult one, spent trying to come to terms with her own identity while still living in the shadows of a mother taken too soon. Her teen years were further complicated by a stepmother who, she says, could not stand the sight of her because of all she represented. She also had to face the continued grieving of adults who saw in Alisa all that had been lost. As a consequence of her confused identity, she spent a lot of time with older people. "I remember my mom's friends being my friends, even though they were much older than I," she says. In a sense, Alisa never had a real childhood, never fit in with her peers at school and church. Her contemporaries didn't seem to have any clue of what life was all about. "They were concerned with all of the wonderfully frivolous things of childhood," she explains, "and I was thinking on a different level. In retrospect, from the age of around ten, I think I was awkward, and was always in a place that the people around me didn't seem to understand. I still get that feeling of not quite fitting in even now, as I approach forty."

Yet being in this awkward place has had its blessings. As a result of her friendships with her mother's friends, and through the influence of her grandparents, Alisa gained much insight about life. Even so, life was difficult, and Alisa left her childhood home as early as she could in order to get away from her troubled family environment. She was accepted into a private Episcopal girls' school and graduated with honors, and not long afterward married a childhood friend. "Brian had been in my life from the time before my mother was killed," explains Alisa, "and he really knew me. He had taken the time to listen to me during all those late-night phone calls about what happens when people die, and what happens when those around you can't move on. He has been the one to understand me many times when I couldn't yet understand myself."

Back before she and Brian were married, Alisa had a dream in which her mother appeared to her and told her that Brian would someday be her husband. In the dream, her mom also told her that although her childhood had been riddled with conflict since her death, Alisa's adulthood would not be. "She said I would find happiness and grow into a beautiful Alisa, not merely the shell of her," Alisa says. "I told Brian about the dream, and, as with all things that are correct and good and meant to be, my mother was right. Brian and I have been married now for twenty years. I think our partnership is a perfect one, because where I'm weak he is strong, and vice versa."

Besides being her soul mate, and her best friend, Brian is also her business partner; together, Alisa and Brian created the Alisa Murray Photography Studio. Actually it is to her uncle – her mother's only brother – that Alisa gives credit for originally inspiring the studio. It was he who first saw that Alisa had a gift. He had given her many pictures of her mother, knowing she instinctively understood that portraits are what you have left once a person is gone. "They are like tiny jewels that are priceless," Alisa says. Her uncle visited her in Houston and taught her the basics of photography, and then gave her a photography assignment. Shortly afterward he had a massive heart attack and died. But he had planted a seed that would not die; one of the portraits that Alisa took as a result of her uncle's photography assignment made the cover of a magazine. It was then that she realized God had sent this man to help set her on the path to her life's work. "No doubt, Mother had a part in it as well," she says, smiling. Over the years the Alisa Murray Photography Studio has grown to be one of the most renowned in the country. "As with all things in my life, I have felt it was a 'God thing,'" Alisa says.

God apparently had even bigger plans for her. After a few years of doing studio work, she heard that one of her friends had been diagnosed with breast cancer. "I asked her for permission to shoot some photographs of her with her daughter, so I would have something to give to her daughter should she not make it through the treatment," Alisa explains. To some that might sound morbid, but to Alisa it is simply realistic. "One thing I must say after having gone through the death of my mother as a child is that I don't assume anyone is going to live to a ripe old age," she says matter-of-factly. "There's always in the back of my mind the possibility that I might not see you again, so I try real hard to say what I need to say. Sometimes this makes people uncomfortable, but I can't have any more regrets. My friends and family know that I love them, and if I were to die suddenly, I will not be unprepared."

Her friend agreed to the photo shoot and, happily, survived the treatments. A few years later Alisa called her and asked her if she knew any other cancer survivors who had children. Alisa wanted to create a breast cancer calendar and fill it with mothers who had survived. Within two weeks, Alisa had a calendar finished, and then, just as she was looking through the layouts of the calendar, a good friend who was also in the media just happened to be in for her sitting. Within another week, Alisa's calendar was on TV. A coincidence? "Ahhh… NO!" Alisa says emphatically. "Again, it was a 'God thing!'" Alisa firmly believes that there are no coincidences in life, and that everything happens for a reason. That calendar, by the way, is now in its eighth year and just recently was featured on the *Today* show.

Perhaps the most surprising of all the ways that Alisa feels God shines through her has been through her writing. In August of 2006 she was asked by a local magazine, *Fort Bend Focus*, to write a feature about her children's rooms, which she had painted. And when I say "painted," I don't mean she just went down to the Home Depot, bought a few gallons of semi-gloss in a trendy color, and slapped it on the walls. Alisa is an artist as well as a photographer, and her kids' rooms reflected her creative skill with the brush – definitely worthy of a feature article. She wrote the piece and supplied the photographs as well, after which the magazine's owner called her personally and said, "We want you to have your own column, and we don't care what you write. Just write!" At first Alisa was a little taken aback since, as she explains it, she was a painter and a photographer, not a writer. However, as she began writing, she soon discovered how easily it came to her. Her column, "Living the Sweet Life," won first place two years in a row for the best original column in Texas.

But it is her artistry with the camera for which Alisa is best known, and over the years, many people have spoken about how her work has touched their lives. From the many women she has captured in various stages of pregnancy and new motherhood… to the old hands of a great-grandparent cradling a new tiny life that will carry on the family name… to the survivors of cancer (both mothers and, as of late, children)… Alisa feels that God has given her the talent to make a difference and leave behind the very things that were most precious to her in childhood: pictures.

She feels that God has given her another gift as well: the gift of herself. "Just as my mother said to me in that dream I had so long ago, he has also allowed me to become, despite my early loss, 'Alisa,' and not just a shell of my mother."

And while we're speaking of gifts, Alisa feels she would be remiss were she to fail to mention that not only do she and her husband Brian work together, but they have also created two beautiful children who, Alisa feels, embody the best characteristics of both of them. "Victoria Ann is as much a likeness of her father as God could have possibly made," Alisa says. "She is musically and academically talented and has a sweet and kind nature. James Edward is the male embodiment of me. I see in his questions about the universe both wisdom and naïveté. He's artistically inclined and has already written and illustrated his first book. He takes pictures and often asks if he can be an artist, painter and writer just like me."

Alisa continues, "God gives us children as gifts. They are given to us to teach us and heal us, inasmuch as we are charged with the awesome responsibility to journey with them through childhood, and to teach them and watch them become everything that God intended them to be. My children are by far my biggest accomplishment. They are the ones who will carry on my life's work even after I am no longer here."

* * * * *

For the past several years Alisa has worked with the many families featured in *Always Hope*, and in her signature style has always sought to capture not just their stories, but their souls as well. Of her work on this project, Alisa says, "Hope is a vital part of living through tragedy, and without it many of the joys that life has to offer are lost. I feel this book is a collection of some of my best artistry. Each person has a very different story of survival, and all are equally important, one no less so than the other. From the loss of a limb, to the near loss of a child, to walking out of and yet bravely back into fire, their stories move you. God works through each of us in so many ways to define who we are to be, and we all have the opportunity to make a difference – even in the wake of tragedy."

She continues, "It has been an awe-inspiring journey to capture the many wonderful people for *Always Hope*. In doing these portraits I would always spend time getting to know each person, and I would receive a vision for what each portrait should portray. As with everything I do, I feel that God is part of the process and my talent as a portrait artist is only fully realized when I allow him to shine his light through me to enable the world to see the beauty and grace in everyone."

For my part, I am glad to call Alisa my friend, and proud to feature her work in this book.
~ *Cindy Cline-Flores*

Alisa and Brian reside in Houston, Texas.
For more information on Alisa's work and column, visit www.alisamurray.com

Cindy Cline-Flores

Afterword

Ihave to admit that my primary motivation for doing this book was that I desperately needed some way of easing the sadness I felt following the death of my older sister, Marion. I needed something to help me make sense of her loss, and even more, something to remind me that life truly is a blessing, even when that blessing is touched by tears.

What I did not expect was to encounter such profound examples of the human spirit's ability to rise above seemingly devastating circumstances, and to find an exquisite sense of joy, wholly untarnished by any challenge.

In the course of putting this book together, I have been blessed with the opportunity to touch – and be touched by – the lives of many remarkable people, all more than willing to share their strength, their wisdom, and their love. They have given me a gift that I will cherish for the rest of my life, one that I only wish I could have shared with Marion. They gave to me the gift of hope, when to all outward appearances, there was only hopelessness. They gave to me a renewal of a faith that is strong enough to transcend any earthly challenges. And they restored in me the sense of wonder that typically defines the world of a child, yet seems too often to fade as we "mature."

Each of us has heard the old adage, "I wept because I had no shoes, until I met a man who had no feet." And each of us has felt the reproach that lies behind those words. After spending time with the people in these stories, the words took on a wholly new meaning for me. Rather than scold myself for wallowing in self-pity, I can honestly see that it is possible to find joy in life, no matter what difficulties that life might throw at us. I have truly met the "man who had no feet," and he was dancing gleefully, running, breathless, into his tomorrows.

My prayer is that I may learn that joyful dance, and that others who read this book may hear that same sweet music, and be enriched by the blessings our Creator has provided.

~ Cindy Cline-Flores

Acknowledgments

First and foremost, I thank all the people who agreed to have their story told in this book. Because of all of you, this book is possible. I have been deeply touched by the grace, courage, and hope that each one of you demonstrate in your lives. Thank you for sharing your private lives with me and allowing me to share your story.

Special thanks go to:

Madeline Westbrook for your guidance.

My sister Deborah Buks for her your, unending support, and for agreeing to share your story of battling Sarcoma.

My brother Byron Cline for your unconditional love for me.

My step-sisters Pat Hamilton, Loretta Diman, Betty McAviney, and Marie Lee for holding the vision.

My niece Kristina Thorson and my nephew Ric Thorson for your love and for sharing your story.

Jay Olivier for connecting me with the Perez family.

Nelia Schrum and Mike Dulevitz for accepting and responding to my seemingly never-ending e-mails, and for your help with research, and for your kindness.

Melissa Wilson at *KRIV Fox 26 News* for help with research.

Alisa Murray (lead photographer); your energy thrust this project off the ground and because of you, there was no turning back!

Ron Kaye and Connie Schmidt for your editing, layout, design, and input for the book…. for your generosity and kindness! I have truly enjoyed working with both of you.

Reverend Howard Caesar for teaching me that life is meant to be good and that with God all things are truly possible…. this book is possible because of this belief!

Diane Caesar for your encouragement, support and love.

Ray Bradbury for your unending support and for writing the Foreword… it means so much!

My mom Helen for your belief in me and in this project.

Roger Leslie for your support.

My son Mark for your patience with me as I spent many nights glued to my computer.

Joe Flores for your patience through the years as I worked on this book, and for the beautiful footage you captured of each of the book participants. Your support means so much!

The staff and my friends at Unity Church for your love and encouragement.

I thank all my friends (you know who you are) and family for your encouragement and belief in this project, especially **Reverend Cheryl Sunday** and **Sharron Border**.

Thank you God, Creator, Spirit
for the gift of life
and the blessing of meeting so many wonderful people…
I am thankful, truly thankful!

Cindy Cline-Flores
Photo by Alisa Murray

Cindy Cline-Flores

About The Author

Cindy Cline-Flores' greatest passion in life is helping others. Even as a small child, while most children her age were focused upon play, Cindy was ever the care-giver. She would come home from school, drop her books on the kitchen table, and rush off to visit the elderly in her neighborhood.

Cindy has worked at Unity Church of Christianity in Houston, Texas for over twenty years in various roles, ultimately serving as Executive Director for twelve years. A few years ago, she chose to reduce her efforts to part-time, in order to devote more time to the care of her mother and her young son Mark, who is the light of her life.

She is a vital part of managing a media production company which she and her husband own.

Cindy is a motivational and keynote speaker, and gives powerful and inspiring lectures and workshops on topics such as Visioning, Empowering Women, Grief Recovery, and Creating a Magnificent Life.

She lives her life with passion and heart, knowing and demonstrating that it is from our hearts as well as our intellect that we can truly heal our suffering and create the kind of world for which we *Always Hope*!

Cindy is available for workshops and presentations, and may be contacted via her website at

www.AlwaysHopeBook.com